LOUISE JORDAN

HOW TO WRITE FOR CHILDREN

and get published

PIATKUS

First published in Great Britain in 1998 by Piatkus Books Ltd
This paperback edition published in 2010 by Piatkus
Reprinted 2010, 2011

A CIP catalogue record for this book
is available from the British Library.

ISBN 978-0-7499-4061-4

Typeset by Phoenix Photosetting, Chatham, Kent
Printed in the UK by CPI Mackays, Chatham ME5 8TD

Papers used by Piatkus are from well-managed forests
and other responsible sources.

MIX
Paper from
responsible sources
FSC® C104740

CONTENTS

With thanks to Marcus for not leaving me when I agreed to do the revised copy of this book!

INTRODUCTION

'Once upon a time' is no time, just as east of the sun and
west of the moon, or the end of the world, is no place. In
reality, however, it means 'at all times, in all places'. It is a
declaration announcing that what you are going to hear is
the truth – both in time and in space. And everyone, be he
king or beggar, needs to hear the truth once in a while at
least.

Erik Haugard on the writing of Hans Christian Andersen

Once upon a time . . .

Once upon a time was – once – how all children's books
started. Today they are more likely to start with first lines such
as:

'"Angus Solomon," sighed Ms Lowry, "Is that a penis
you've drawn in your exercise book?"'

(*Bumface* by Morris Gleitzman)

'I've never told this story to anyone because when I was
twelve I swore an oath in blood that I would never tell it.'

(*Time Bomb* by Nigel Hinton)

'Old Granny Greengrass had her finger chopped off in the
butcher's when she was buying half a leg of lamb.'

(*The Peppermint Pig* by Nina Bawden)

'I am drowning in the roaring silence. I am drowning. I'm going to die.'

(*Pig Heart Boy* by Malorie Blackman)

"'Are you aware," said Mr Simkin to Mrs Simkin one morning, "that the bathtub's halfway down the stairs."'

(*Mr Simkin's Bathtub* by Linda Allen)

If you hanker after the days of 'Once upon a Time', perhaps this book is not for you. If, on the other hand, you are gripped by power and immediacy of the first lines above and can sense excitement to come, read on.

WHY A CHILDREN'S BOOK?

'Everyone who has ever been a child, had a child, seen a child or heard a child thinks that he or she can write a children's book.'

So began a rather disparaging article on 'wannabe' children's writers in the *New York Times* a few years ago: the implication being that children's publishing should function as some sort of exclusive club where new members are all but barred.

Most major children's publishers receive well over 1000 unsolicited submissions every year. Out of these 'slush piles' (I hate that term!) only a very few will make it through to publication. Some publishers may take one or two completely new authors a year, others none at all. This isn't so discouraging when put in context. Even a relatively large children's publisher will only publish, in total, around 200 books a year; and you have to consider that many of these titles are either reprints, or commissions from already established authors, rather than new titles.

So children's publishing is a fairly exclusive club but, whilst new members may not be welcomed with open arms, they are certainly not blackballed. To gain membership, however, it is important to examine why you want to write a children's book in the first place.

Here are a few reasons that have been stated to me by would-be children's authors over the years:

'I really want to write an adult bestseller, but I thought I'd stand more chance with a children's book to start with.'

No! This must be the number one worst reason for choosing to write for children. For a start, writing a children's book is not *easier* than writing an adult book, merely *different*. Many potential children's writers feel that simplicity of vocabulary is the key: it isn't. What *is* needed is a clarity of vision, and this is harder to achieve than you might think. Second, it is just as hard to get a children's book taken on by a publisher as it is to find a publisher for adult writing. Third, you're never going to write a good children's book unless you are totally committed to the task in hand – unless you really *want* and *need* to write it.

'I want to make lots of money like Allan Ahlberg and J. K. Rowling.'

No! Unless you make it to the very top, writing for children doesn't pay well. So don't give up the day job – not yet anyway.

'My children/nieces/nephews/grandchildren love my stories and say I should get them published.'

No! That is – 'No, that's not a good reason,' not – 'No, they don't like your stories.' They probably *do*, very much, but they're reacting to *you*, the person they love, as much as to the story itself. Don't get me wrong, it's a good starting point; it means that you can communicate successfully with children and hold their attention. Just remember that your children/nieces/nephews/ grandchildren aren't the public at large, neither are they publishers. To make the leap from storyteller extraordinaire to published writer is extremely tough. Keep hold of that first inspired spark – but let go of the stories themselves. Until you've finished reading this book, at any rate.

'There's nothing but rubbish published these days and I want to write the sort of books I used to enjoy as a child.'

Fine. Write the sort of books that you used to enjoy – but don't expect them to be published. Those books you enjoyed – the classics – *are* still being published, but if you think that anything more contemporary is rubbish then you haven't been looking in the right places. Anne Fine, Jacqueline Wilson, Malorie Blackman, Michael Morpurgo, Jeremy Strong, Anthony

Horowitz, Melvin Burgess ... the list of wonderfully exciting and original authors goes on. Children's literature is scaling new heights from year to year.

'I've got a good idea.'
That certainly helps. A good idea is an essential starting point and a good idea that would only suit a young market is certainly a valid reason for writing specifically for children. Be warned though: is it *really* a good idea? Is it a book demanding to be born? Or have you got one eye on lucrative merchandising contracts and the other on potential television rights? If so, you probably haven't got a good idea at all. What you have got is a leaky business proposition that won't fool a children's publisher – or the children themselves.

'I want to write for me.'
Yes! It's as simple as that. The best children's writers are writing for themselves – not the child in themselves. Children's writer, Eleanor Farjeon, once advised would-be writers: 'Write only what *you* enjoy writing. Don't write down for children, don't try to be on their level, don't think there is a special tone they will respond to, don't be afraid of words or of things you feel children can't grasp. When you write for children, be yourself.'

Good advice. Writers may exploit emotions and thoughts remembered from their own childhood, but the stories they tell will be firmly entrenched in their own lives *today*.

'I want to pass on things that I have learned to the next generation.'
Yes – another good reason for writing for children. But don't forget, if you try to 'preach' too obviously through your writing you will lose sight of your story. And in children's fiction the story *must* remain the most important factor.

James Watson, writer of children's historical fiction, says that when he first started writing he wrote to entertain, to inform and (possibly) educate. He soon discovered, though, that this left out 'the crucial role of being in there; of being it. For a split second, if the illusion has been well-enough staged, the reader is the experience.'

Which brings us to the final, and best, reason for writing for children:

'I want to give them a reading experience they'll never forget.'
Yes! Yes! Yes! Who can forget the first book they ever read? The thrill of watching a child discover a marvellous book for the first time? As the redoubtable Miss Jean Brodie was fond of quoting, in the film *The Prime of Miss Jean Brodie*: 'Give me a child in her formative years and I'll make her mine for life.'

Bearing this in mind, it is vital therefore that writers for children take their craft seriously and tackle issues in a sensitive and responsible manner. Childhood experiences have a direct link with adult behaviour and so, to a certain extent, the books a child is reading today are shaping the attitudes and society of tomorrow.

THE CHILDREN'S BOOK MARKET AND THE NEW WRITER

Harry Potter and the Half-Blood Prince (Bloomsbury), the sixth instalment of J. K. Rowling's blockbuster series, took the UK children's book market to new heights in 2005. The children's edition of the book ended the year having sold almost 2.9 million copies. The phenomenal effect of Rowling's latest book saw it account for 11.2% of £243.7m children's book sales.

Children's literature has been one of the most resilient areas of publishing, tending to withstand economic recessions. The Harry Potter books proved to be a driver of growth in the children's book market as a whole, with general children's book sales rising by 17.3% in one year alone. Children's books now represent a staggering 15% or so of the Total Consumer Market. In a recent online survey conducted by *The Book Magazine,* three children's writers appeared in the top ten most venerated names in modern literature – J. K. Rowling (at the top), Terry Pratchett and Phillip Pullman.

Schools and libraries have provided a solid source of sales. Figures for 2005, compiled by Public Lending Rights (PLR), show that, while library borrowing as a whole continues to decline, children's writing, and teenage fiction in particular, shows strong growth. The current Children's Laureate, Jacqueline Wilson, is the most borrowed author in UK libraries for the third year running and was the only UK writer (adult or children's) to notch up over 2 million loans. Indeed, out of six writers who notched up over 1 million loans, three were writing for children – namely Jacqueline Wilson, Mick Inkpen and Janet & Allan Ahlberg. Roald Dahl also features in the top ten.

UK Public Lending Rights Registrar, James Parker, has declared that libraries are loath to cut back on children's titles since they support the adult readers and borrowers of the future. Even people who rarely read in their own childhood are now quite likely to buy books for their children. Books are generally seen as a 'good thing'. The initial novelty impact of satellite/cable television and video and computer games has worn off a little – certainly with parents – and the general feeling is that children should be offered a more stimulating alternative. This is clearly illustrated by the increasing number of reading initiatives being introduced into the schools curriculum and young people's lives in general. Initiatives such as World Book Day, Children's Book Week and the Summer Reading Challenge.

However, all schools, whether private or state, have limited resources these days and parents cannot necessarily rely on them – or on reading initiatives – to provide their children with the best choice of reading material. Even if a child is lucky enough to attend a well-financed school, parents are encouraged to back up reading skills taught in school, at home, by taking an interest in books and, where budgets allow, by buying children's books for themselves.

As well as this, children's publishing is now attracting more media attention than ever before. Production teams working in television and film have long since woken up to the fact that just because a piece of fiction is written for children doesn't mean that adults can't enjoy it as well. Books such as *Madame Doubtfire, The Sheep Pig, A Series of Unfortunate Events,* the *Harry Potter* series and *The Chronicles of Narnia* are all good, pacey, interesting stories with a wide-ranging appeal, irrespective of the age of the reader. It doesn't surprise me in the least that all of them attracted huge adult audiences when turned into films. Similarly,

Julie Burchills' book *Sugar Rush* made compulsive, risqué, television, transmitted, as it was, after the 9pm 'watershed'.

Celebrities, too, are vying for the opportunity to write for the children's market, drawing ever more attention to the children's book world. Madonna has written a series of beautifully produced Picture Books, Kylie Minogue has given us a child-friendly version of her life, *Kylie: The Showgirl Princess,* Paul McCartney has published the wittily titled *High in the Clouds: An Urban Furry Tail* and Ricky Gervais offers something a little different for the bedtime story market – the *Flanimals* books featuring a collection of spectacularly ugly creatures.

A general growth in prominence of the children's book market can only mean more openings and greater opportunities for those who want to write for children. Sifting through the slush pile is extremely labour-intensive. Yet most publishers carry on with this procedure for fear of missing the next bestseller. The list of classic books that have been missed by one publisher and picked up by another is endless. The most famous, recent example is J. K. Rowling's first book, *Harry Potter and the Philosopher's Stone*, which was turned down by countless publishers before finally finding a home with Bloomsbury. Author G. P. Taylor became so disillusioned by rejection that he published *Shadowmancer* himself before Faber finally snapped it up, making him a millionaire.

Contrary to public opinion, children's publishers are extremely keen to find promising new writers. Recently, Lion Children's Books even went as far as launching a 'hunting for an author' competition with a £1000 prize and promise of publication.

But it *is* a very competitive market and writers approaching publishers with material should be aware that their manuscript must display enormous strength and real sales potential to warrant anything other than a polite rejection.

ABOUT THIS BOOK

So how do you learn? How do you make absolutely sure that you are going to get it right? Gone are the days when editors had the time to 'build' authors from scratch. That job has now fallen to the literary agent, but agents won't usually consider representing an author, and spending valuable time working with them, unless they have at least one book under their belt.

In this book, I have tried to pass on everything I know about writing for children, picked up from many years in the business as an editor, writer and reader. I have tried to put myself in the place of someone who wakes up one morning and thinks, or, better still, *knows* that 'I want to write a children's book' but doesn't have the first clue where to start.

You *can* do it. But you do have to know what you're doing. This book provides a step-by-step guide: Part One deals with the market; Part Two with technique; and Part Three with all the practical details that you need to consider once you are ready to approach publishers.

Treat this book rather as you would a correspondence course. Start at the beginning with Lesson One and progress through to the end of the book. Some of the information you will need to know before you can write your first word — some of it you may never need — but it is important to absorb it *all*.

There are exercises at the end of most chapters. Try to do as many as possible. There are many different types of writing for children and the exercises will help you discover which ones are suited to your particular style of creativity.

So imagine: Imagine you are me, sitting at my desk. The phone rings.

'I want to write a children's book,' says the tentative voice on the other end. 'Where do I start?'

Right here. Right now. Read on ...

I

KNOW YOUR MARKET

CHAPTER ONE

THE
PICTURE BOOK

Every book has to start somewhere and I'm starting this one at the youngest end of the children's book market. For those of you who also think that I've started with the easiest option, think again.

> *'There's nothing to those picture books. Money for old rope.'*
> *'There's only a few words on each page. Wouldn't take a second to write.'*
> *'The art's all in the pictures. The writing doesn't matter.'*

These are comments that I have heard made, over the years, about the children's Picture Book. They are understandable comments but they all fall way short of the truth. The Picture Book is, in reality, the hardest format to choose if you want to break into the children's market: the hardest to write, and definitely the hardest to sell.

WHAT IS A PICTURE BOOK?

Let's first examine what we actually mean by a 'Picture Book'; there does seem to be some confusion over the term. Some writers are adamant that they have written a Picture Book when, in fact, they have written an illustrated children's story. There is a difference.

A Picture Book is a large format storybook for the 0–6-year-old age group. Illustrated in full colour, it has a pre-specified number of pages that is never less than twenty-four and usually not more than forty. It is important to realise that *all* the pages are included in this calculated number, including the front and back covers. The other point to take on board is that the total number of pages must be divisible by eight – twenty-four, thirty-two, forty etc. Generally speaking, the twenty-four-page book is for the younger child (0–2 years), the thirty-two-pager for the middle section (3–4 years) and the forty-pager for the older child (5–6 years).

Picture Books are rarely more than 1000 words in length and are usually a good deal shorter than this. When Pat Hutchins first wrote *Rosie's Walk*, the text, as she admits, went 'on and on'. After a lot of work, she cut it down to just thirty-two words. It works brilliantly.

Rosie's Walk is a book for reading aloud, but there are a number of different styles of Picture Book. There are early-learning books: alphabet books, nursery rhymes, word books, etc. There are short-story books, books for reading aloud, books for reading alone, books to be looked at, participation books . . . the list goes on!

As a new writer, don't try rhyming texts. These are difficult to translate and, as you read on, you will discover that publishers ideally like to be able to sell the 'rights' of your book abroad.

Novelty books are out as well. These include lift-the-flap books, bath books, board books, pop-up books etc. The manufacture of such books is expensive and no publisher will take the financial risk involved with an untried author. These books tend to be specially commissioned or originated in-house.

So why is it such a difficult area?

For a new Picture Book to be taken on, the publisher first has to be absolutely sure that another country (such as America) will be prepared to publish it as well. This is called a co-edition; by organising co-editions, a publishing house is able to guarantee a much larger initial print run. This, in turn, brings down the unit cost of the book and makes it economically viable. Even with today's new digital technology and the concept of 'print on demand', the cost of producing a full-colour book to sell in just one country is, quite frankly, prohibitive.

Selling the idea of a co-edition to foreign publishers often takes place at the international book fairs in Frankfurt, London and Bologna. Frankfurt and London deal in general publishing, whereas Bologna is geared up specifically for children's publishing.

Once your Picture Book has been accepted, in principle, by a British publisher, they may well ask you if they can present your idea at these book fairs. Usually, you will be offered some sort of contract to cover this situation and sometimes you will be offered a development fee. It is impossible to be categoric about the amount an author will be offered – it will vary from publisher to publisher. Obviously, larger publishers can afford to offer a bigger development fee, with smaller publishers offering much less, if anything at all!

Whether your publisher is able to interest a foreign publisher often depends on the subject matter and the tone of the book. Some genres, particularly humour, work well in one country but do not translate well elsewhere, because of cultural differences. Interest will also depend on whether the foreign publisher feels that the author and illustrator have a proven track record.

At this point, I sense that, all over the country, pens and pencils are being hurled across rooms and computers and word processors are being turned off. Pick them up! Turn them back on. Don't despair! It is hard to break into this very competitive sector of the children's market, but it is by no means impossible.

The highly successful children's author, Malorie Blackman, initially found success with her Picture Book *That New Dress*, which was so good it received offers from two publishers simultaneously. Daniel Postgate, another acclaimed children's author, broke into the market with his Picture Book *Kevin Saves the World*. And these are just two examples that spring immediately to mind.

How do I start?

When writing a Picture Book, you have to first decide whether or not your idea is suited to the Picture Book style. Is the plot fairly simple? Is there plenty of scope for a wide variety of illustrations?

Winnie the Witch by Korky Paul and Valerie Thomas is an excellent example of a book perfectly suited to its format:

Winnie the Witch lived in a black house in the forest. The house was black on the outside and black on the inside. The carpets were black. The chairs were black. The bed was black and it had black sheets and black blankets. Even the bath was black.

Winnie lived in her black house with her cat, Wilbur. He was black too. And that is how the trouble began.

The 'trouble' is that Winnie can't see her cat and so she is always falling over him. The book tells the tale of how Winnie changes her black cat first to green, then multi-coloured, and then, when nothing works out, back to black. To get round the problem of not being able to see him, she finally puts a colour spell on her house:

Now instead of a black house, she had a yellow house with a red room and a red door. The chairs were white with red and white cushions. The carpet was green with pink roses. The bed was blue, with pink and white sheets and pink blankets. The bath was a gleaming white.

The plot of this book is intriguingly simple and the text gives plenty of scope for Korky Paul's vibrant illustrations.

This particular book is for the 3–5-year-old and falls to thirty-two pages. However, the author has less than this to work with. Pages one and thirty-two are the front and back outside covers; pages two and thirty-one are the inside covers; page three is blank; page four contains copyright details (ISBN number, publisher's address, publication date etc.), page five is the title page; and page thirty is a blank end page. The story actually starts on page six and ends on page twenty-nine . . . leaving only twenty-four pages for text and illustrations in a thirty-two page book (sixteen in a twenty-four pager)!

Let's assume that you have an idea that is best suited to a twenty-four-page format. Follow a few simple steps in order to construct your story:

1 Write out your text in a straight 'chunk'.
2 Take another piece of paper and list the numbers six to twenty-one down one side. Then work out how your text is

going to divide up on a page-by-page basis and make a note of this by each number.

3 Take a large sheet of paper and map out a layout chart for a twenty-four-page book, following the template shown in our illustration. You should end up with twelve halved rectangles.

4 Sketch out, roughly, how you see your layout working. Write in the text on each page showing where it will fall, show where the illustrations will fall (but don't produce illustrations at this stage), where your double-spreads (illustrations and text spread over two adjacent pages) will fall, and so on.

When carrying out this exercise, try to make your layout as varied as possible. It does not necessarily have to follow the traditional format of text on one side and illustration on the other. Some pages could be split into several smaller sections, and some pages may require no text at all.

One good way of ensuring the correct balance of words and pictures is to take a Picture Book that you feel works well and resembles the type of book you are trying to write, then work backwards, producing a layout chart by following the example of the published book. By analysing the chart it will be clear how the author has structured the book. Copy that same structure for your own work. This is *not* plagiarism. You will (hopefully) end up with a very different story. But until you are more experienced it is an excellent discipline and guide.

Bear in mind the juxtaposition of words and pictures. In many Picture Books, the story is told as much by the pictures as by the words – but it needs an interesting combination of both to work. Children's illustrator, Korky Paul, likens the process to a movie:

'As the drawer you are not only the cinematographer but also the director, the casting agent, the costume designer and responsible for the locations, lighting, props and continuity! The text is the soundtrack and it's that special combination between words and pictures that makes for good storytelling in a Picture Book. As in a movie, neither can exist properly on their own.'

Take Pat Hutchins' *Rosie's Walk*:

Rosie the hen went for a walk, across the yard, around the pond, over the haycock, past the mill, through the fence, under the beehives, and got back in time for dinner.

On their own, the words are not particularly exciting. Combined with witty and appealing illustrations, however, they become loaded with humour, as we watch the fox unsuccessfully stalking Rosie and having mishap after amusing mishap.

What about the illustrations?

Pat Hutchins is a writer *and* an illustrator. But this is a rare breed indeed! If you honestly feel that you can both write well and illustrate well then by all means have a go. Otherwise, I would suggest approaching a publisher with the text only. Make a few suggestions for illustrations but stress that it is the idea and words that you are presenting.

It is not a good idea to approach a publisher with a complete package – in other words with your own text allied to an illustrator's drawings, or vice versa. A publisher might like the text but not the illustrations – or the illustrations but not the text – but will be put off the whole concept because you have presented it as a team effort.

An illustrator is better advised to approach children's design departments direct with a few samples of his/her work. All design departments hold 'banks' of illustrators and are always pleased to discover new, talented illustrators to take onto their books.

If you are that rare writer/illustrator there is no need to spend hours perfecting colour artwork to go with your text. It's better to send a couple of finished colour pages and the rest as roughs. *Never* send original artwork. Colour photocopies might not be a true representation of an artist's work, but they are quite sufficient to enable a publisher to make a judgement.

If you are not an illustrator but nonetheless have very set ideas as to how your book should look, it is perfectly acceptable to say, in your covering letter, something along the lines of: 'I see my book being illustrated in the style of (name illustrator), but I am happy to work with an illustrator of your choice.'

How do I present my work?

In many ways it doesn't matter how you present your work to publishers so long as it is neat and legible. It is also important to make your presentation look as professional as possible. You have to convince the editor that you are not just another amateur wannabe writer: you know what you're doing and it is therefore worth the editor's while to look carefully at your submission.

I would suggest typing out the text on single-sided white A4 paper, showing the page breaks. For example, the original text submission for *Not Now, Bernard* by David McKee might have read:

Page 6: 'Hello, Dad,' said Bernard.
Page 7: 'Not now, Bernard,' said his father.
Page 8: 'Hello, Mum,' said Bernard.
Page 9: 'Not now, Bernard,' said his mother.

And so on, through to page 29 where the book ends (it is a thirty-two-page Picture Book – remember these often don't start until page 6).

It's also helpful to present a 'dummy' or a 'mock-up' to go with the straight typed version of the text. A dummy is easily made by taking however many pages you need of A3 paper (A4 can be used, but you don't end up with a lot of space to work with), stacking them together, folding the whole stack in half and then sewing or stapling down the centrefold. For a twenty-four-page book you will need twelve sheets; for a thirty-two-page book sixteen; and so on. The outside sheet (i.e. the sheet that forms the front and back cover) can be replaced with coloured paper but this isn't really necessary.

You now have a homemade blank book in which you write the text and brief descriptions (or sketches, if you can draw) of possible illustrations. Lauren Child's books (*Charlie & Lola*, for example) are classic examples of how important design is when planning a Picture Book. She uses a very 'busy' style, often splitting her pages as far as illustrations are concerned and varying the way in which the text is written in terms of layout, font and size. Even if, as the author, you are unable to draw, it is possible to use the dummy to show how the text can be worked to maximum effect. I would suggest writing the text in one colour ink and the illustrative description in another, for the sake of clarity. The dummy isn't vital – in David McKee's *Not Now,*

Bernard it may not have been necessary at all as he deliberately sticks to a very classic format with the words at the bottom of each page – but it does show the publisher that you can visualise your own work.

What about the writing?

Remember that a child will often want to hear the same Picture Book read out loud over and over again. This means that your text has to have a rhythm that will leave both the listener and the reader feeling satisfied every time.

Take the classic children's Picture Book *We're Going on a Bear Hunt* by Michael Rosen and Helen Oxenbury. The author cleverly uses a mixture of rhythm, repetition and onomatopoeic words to convey a text that is both poetic and lyrical. Nothing very much happens in the book but the simple text follows the same format, which makes it perfect for reading aloud.

> We're going on a bear hunt.
> We're going to catch a big one.
> What a beautiful day!
> We're not scared. [page 8]
> Uh-uh! Grass!
> We can't go over it.
> We can't go under it.
> Oh no!
> We've got to go through it! [page 9]

The words on page 8 are repeated again and again on pages 12, 16, 20, 24 and 28. Each page that follows has the family battling through different mediums – a river, mud, a forest, a snowstorm and a cave. Again the words on page 9 are repeated, each time with very slight variations.

> Uh-uh! A river!
> A deep cold river.
> We can't go over it.
> We can't go under it.
> Oh no!
> We've got to go through it! [page 13]

And,

> Uh-uh! Mud!
> Thick oozy mud.
> We can't go over it.
> We can't go under it.
> Oh no!
> We've got to go through it! [page 17]

Just as rhythm is very important in Picture Books, a rhyming text is very unimportant. As mentioned above, it isn't advisable, in any case, to write a rhyming text. The fact of the matter is, it isn't the rhyming that's important, it's the way the words sound. So still using *We're Going on a Bear Hunt* as our example text:

> Quick! Back through the cave! Tiptoe! Tiptoe! Tiptoe!
> Back through the snowstorm! Hoooo wooooo! Hoooo wooooo!
> Back through the forest! Stumble trip! Stumble trip! Stumble trip!
> Back through the mud! Squelch squerch! Squelch squerch!
> Back through the river! Splash splosh! Spash splosh! Splash splosh!
> Back through the grass! Swishy swashy! Swishy swashy!
> [pages 34–35]

There is a compelling feeling to the words themselves that brings the story alive.

The best Picture Books are good stories in themselves. But they usually contain a message as well. *Not Now, Bernard* is, in theory, a book about a little boy who is eaten by a monster; but it is also a book about the angry feelings a child may experience when ignored by his parents. Similarly, *Something Else* by Kathryn Cave and Chris Riddell is a poignantly simple tale about . . . well, Something Else. "'You don't belong here,' they said. "You're not like us. You're something else.'"

The combination of Kathryn Cave's text and Chris Riddell's illustrations brings the character of *Something Else* alive and teaches the reader that it's OK to be different: 'They were different, but they got along. And when something turned up that really was weird-looking [a perfectly 'normal' human child!], they didn't say he wasn't like them and he didn't belong there. They moved right up and made room for him too.'

Creators of children's television characters often approach editors thinking that their ideas will translate into saleable Picture Books. This is seldom the case. TV cartoon characters appeal in a very immediate, superficial way; a good Picture Book will, hopefully, have more depth and be remembered. It is much more likely that strong children's Picture Book characters will be lifted by television executives looking for good programme ideas, so a final point to remember is that it is now more important than ever to come up with a strong commercial idea as well as great writing.

Picture Book Exercise

- Think of your own original idea for a Picture Book.
- Write out the text without worrying about pagination.
- Find a published Picture Book that you feel works well.
- Create a layout chart for it, noting how the story and pictures are structured.
- Using your own idea and text, copy the layout, trying to keep to approximately the same number of words.
- Make up a dummy and try out your book on a young child. (To maintain their interest it is sometimes a nice idea to ask them to 'fill in' the pictures.)

CHAPTER TWO

YOUNG FICTION

Young Fiction covers a wide range of ages, ranging from around five years, up to eight or nine years. These books are specifically targeted at children who are either just starting to read – or gaining confidence in reading – yet are too young to handle full-length General Fiction. They are always illustrated – sometimes in black and white and sometimes colour.

There will, inevitably, be some overlap in age range with the Picture Book market. However, Young Fiction books are very much normal size, not large format. There is also no need for the author to concern themselves with either the illustrations or the page count. The emphasis here is on strong stories and word count rather than layout and visuality.

The length of Young Fiction titles varies hugely depending on whether a book is targeted at the lower end of the age scale (5–6 years) or the higher end (8–9 years). As far as word counts are concerned, texts can range from as little as 1000 words to as many as 10,000 words for older readers. Allan Ahlberg's *Happy Families* books are very much at the shorter end of this market, Jeremy Strong's books come somewhere in the middle, whereas Humphrey Carpenter's *Mr Majeika* books are more substantial and demanding reads.

Historically, Young Fiction has been one of the easier areas of the children's book market to break into. However, sadly, this is no longer the case. Because of the illustrative content of these books, they are expensive to produce – particularly if in full colour – and, as a result, most publishers prefer to use established authors who they are confident will push up sales. However, while stand-alone Young Fiction is now, almost, a 'no-go' area, there are two areas in this versatile sector that still offer opportunities to the new writer. These are Series Reads and Series Fiction.

WHAT ARE SERIES READS?

'A serious read?' queried one of my authors, mishearing me as I described the next stage up from the Picture Book. I had, in fact, said 'a *Series* Read' but, in many ways, the author was right. Series Reads are a more *serious* read than Picture Books – not in quality, but in quantity.

Don't let the word 'series' fool you. This is not, as the name suggests and many potential authors believe, the publisher's way of extracting a series of books from one particular writer. Indeed, nothing puts off an editor more than a new, untried writer claiming they are working on 'a series' before they have had even one book accepted!

You will hear this section of the Series Read market called a number of different things: Series Readers; Picture Storybooks; First Storybooks; Reading Series; and so on. It's confusing, but don't worry – it all boils down to the same thing in the end.

To all intents and purposes, Series Reads follow exactly the same formats as stand-alone Young Fiction, i.e. they are aimed at children who are just learning to read and are illustrated. The only difference is that with Series Reads, publishers group titles together under a series name and target them at very specific age levels. Categories tend to be beginner or first readers, developing or newly confident readers and confident or fluent readers.

Each different series will conform to an easily identifiable look and length, and will have a consistent level of language and vocabulary, even though they may be by different authors. The idea is that if children find a book they like, they will want to go on to read other titles in the same series, and these titles will be immediately identifiable on the bookshelves.

The Series Read market is an interesting one – and certainly one of the more receptive as far as a new author is concerned.

There are two reasons for this. First, most series are ongoing and publishers need to publish a certain number of new titles every year to fulfil the requirements of each series.

Second, the Series Read book is marketed using the title of a particular series, as opposed to the name of an author. This makes it easier – and less risky financially as far as the publisher is concerned – to promote new authors, as once a series is established it will go on selling no matter who writes for it.

All mainstream publishers produce Series Readers of one kind or another. Rather like the Three Bears, some produce big ones, some produce medium-sized ones and some produce small ones. Knowing who, exactly, produces what is usually the most bewildering aspect of this market for the new author.

Tips on researching the market are dealt with in detail later in this book, but below is a chart listing the requirements of various different publishers. Please note that this was accurate at the time of going to press and that not all the publishers listed accept unsolicited manuscripts. The series are listed in order of word counts starting with the shortest titles.

Series Name	Word Count	Age Range	Publisher
Tadpoles	70 words	4–6	Franklin Watts
Leapfrog	180 words	4–6	Franklin Watts
Hopscotch	350–400 words	5–7	Franklin Watts
Green Bananas	500 words	4 +	Egmont Books
Blue Bananas	1000 words	5 +	Egmont Books
Chameleons	1200 words	5–7	A & C Black
I Am Reading	1200 words	5–7	Kingfisher
Crunchies	1000–1500 words	5–7	Orchard Books
Colour Crunchies	1000–1500 words	5–7	Orchard Books
Walker Stories	1800 words	5 +	Walker Books
Red Bananas	2000 words	6 +	Egmont Books
Colour Young Puffin	2500 words	5–7	Puffin Boooks
Tiger Cubs	1000–3000 words	5–8	Andersen Press
Tigers	3000–5000 words	6–9	Andersen Press
Super Crunchies	5000 words	7–9	Orchard Books
Racing Reads	8000 words	7–9	Walker Books

With the exception of the very youngest Readers, most of these books are divided into chapters; the shorter the total word length, the shorter the chapters.

To make them more attractive for the young child, they can be illustrated with a mixture of colour illustrations and black-and-white line drawings. Sometimes they are illustrated in full colour throughout.

Now, if you are getting all hot and bothered at the very mention of illustrations because you can't even draw pin-people, calm down and take a deep breath. Illustrations for the Series Reader market are there only to add interest to the text and to make the book seem more accessible for the child. Unlike when writing a Picture Book, the author does *not* have to consider illustrations when coming up with an idea. Publishers will happily match an illustrator with your text, should it be accepted.

Do consider which series your story is best suited to. Each series has a slightly different 'feel' and the only way to get to grips with the differences between them is by reading as many as possible. Series Reads can have storylines ranging from the modern fairytale, to everyday events, to science fiction, to animal adventure. It doesn't really matter what you decide to write about – so long as the style and content suits the Reader series you are targeting.

Vocabulary must be simple, clear and unsophisticated. Plots must be action-based and uncluttered, and writing style should be pacey and direct. The one thing to bear in mind when writing for any Series Reads is that humour, whether zany or more gentle, is a key element for this age group.

Writing the Reader: Exercises

- Pay a visit to the children's section of your local library or bookshop and study some of the Series Reads mentioned in this chapter.
- Think of your own idea for a Series Read.
- Based on what you have read, try to establish what age group your idea is for and how long (in words) it will be.
- With a particular Reading Series in mind, plot out your book chapter by chapter, remembering to take into account the number of words in each chapter.

Series Fiction

When I talk about Series Fiction, I mean literally that – a series of fiction books with the same generic title. They can be written by one author, by lots of authors or, alternatively, by a number of different authors writing under a single pseudonym. The highly successful *Animal Ark* series, published by HodderHeadline, written by Lucy Daniels, is a good example of Series Fiction.

Although Series Fiction titles are published by the same publishers who produce Readers, they are usually commissioned in a different way. This is because they often come from packagers.

What on earth are 'packagers', I hear you ask? You'll hear more about them when I talk about non-fiction later in the book. However, as far as Series Fiction is concerned, a packager is a company that comes up with the idea for a particular series and then persuades a publisher to take it on.

It works along the following lines: Bill and Ben of Flowerpot Men International (a UK packager) have just finished doing a presentation to the Editorial Director of Gosling Books (a big children's publisher). They have demonstrated to the Editorial Director that there is a gap in the pony books market for girls of around 8–10 years. They have suggested, to fill this gap, a series of short books about a family who run a riding stables in a London suburb. Each book would tell the story of a different adventure set in and around the stables. The heroine of the series would be Pamela, the daughter of the family who own the stables.

'Great stuff!' says the Editorial Director. 'We'll do it.' (Of course, real life isn't usually like that. In real life, the Editorial Director would probably say, 'I'll get back to you next week,' and six months later, Bill and Ben would be none the wiser.)

So Bill and Ben go away and put together a proper brief, which they will send out to agents saying they are looking for writers. The briefs for this type of Series Fiction can vary but they are usually fairly specific. Bill and Ben would say what sort of girl Pamela is (it could even describe what she looks like), give details of any family and friends they want included in the stories, describe what the riding stables is like (where it is, how big it is, how many ponies etc.) and would go on to outline the plots of the first few books.

Any interested authors would then submit a sample and, if this was satisfactory, would be commissioned to write the entire book. This will be edited by Bill and Ben and presented to the publisher as a complete 'package'.

Many authors are not keen on doing this type of work. Some feel that, because the idea has already been thought through in some detail, it would not be 'their' work in the true sense of the word. Other authors find the discipline of working to someone else's brief too demanding. Some even believe that such a commercial form of fiction is demeaning, and writing under a pseudonym, insulting.

Personally, I think that writing Series Fiction is excellent experience for the new writer; it can provide a steady income in an otherwise uncertain market. Top children's agent, Lesley Hadcroft of Laurence Pollinger, calls it 'gas bill money'. However, it is, unfortunately, a fairly inaccessible market as far as the new writer is concerned. How do you, as a new writer, get to hear about new Series Fiction projects? You most likely won't have an agent until you have had a few books published, and editors working on these projects tend to rely on agents for their writers.

There are a number of sensible steps you can take to try to find this kind of work. First, look out for new Series Fiction titles in the shops. If you see a series developing, check out the publishing (biblio) details on the opening (prelim) pages. Even if you can't work out who the packager is, this page will give you the name of the publisher. Drop them a line, with a sample of writing and details of any relevant experience, asking if they're looking for new authors for that particular series.

Alternatively, you could always try approaching packagers direct in the same way. There is a list of packagers who deal in children's books in *The Children's Writers' and Artists' Yearbook*.

Working Partners is one of the best known packagers for Series Fiction and, since 1995, they have created some of the most recognised series in children's fiction. Their series are published by all the leading English-language publishers and include *Animal Ark*, *Heartland* and, more recently, *Rainbow Magic* and *Warriors*.

Just to show how successful this particular sector of the market can be, *Rainbow Magic*, Working Partners' young fairy fiction series, now has sales of five million copies in the UK and Commonwealth. Translation rights have been licensed in seventeen territories and that list looks set to grow. Similarly, *Animal Ark*, now with its own Classics list in the UK, has sold over fifteen million copies worldwide. Initially commissioned as a six-book series, *Animal Ark* and its spin-off series now comprise over 100 titles for readers aged 5 to 12.

Series Fiction: Exercise

- Pay a visit to the children's section of your local bookshop or library and try to identify as many Series Fiction titles as possible.
- Study the opening pages of each title in the Series carefully and try to work out whether the Series is written by a single author, or by a number of different authors.
- Check out the Working Partners website (workingpartners ltd.co.uk) and select a series that appeals to you. Now think of a new idea for another book in the same series, using the same setting and characters.
- Write the first chapter and then do a brief chapter-by-chapter breakdown for the rest of the book.

CHAPTER THREE

WRITING FICTION FOR THE EDUCATIONAL MARKET

The good news is that this is a far more accessible area of the children's book market, as far as the new writer is concerned, than it was when I wrote the original version of this book. Walk into any large bookshop and the children's area sees whole bays devoted to education books.

If you do decide to explore this very demanding, but highly rewarding market, you will straight away come up against three very specific terms. These are 'National Curriculum', 'the Literacy Hour' and 'Phonics'. For those of you who currently have children of school-going age or are, perhaps, already involved in education, these terms will be all too familiar and it may even seem strange to you that they need any explanation at all. However, for those of you who perhaps don't have children of your own or who have taken to writing a little later in life, the modern educational system and its dictates probably seems vast and confusing. It needn't be.

WHAT IS THE NATIONAL CURRICULUM?

The National Curriculum was introduced into England, Wales and Northern Ireland as a nationwide curriculum for primary and secondary state schools. Its purpose is to ensure that state schools of all Local Education Authorities (LEAs) have a common curriculum and that certain basic material is covered by all pupils. It does not, technically, apply to Independent Schools, although, for most of them, it has made sense to follow similar guidelines.

The curriculum is divided up into four key stages: Key Stage 1 (ages 5–7), Key Stage 2 (ages 7–11), Key Stage 3 (ages 11–14) and Key Stage 4 (ages 14–16). Some publishers have already taken on board that the National Curriculum can be a confusing area for many parents. For example, Egmont are introducing information into their *Banana Books* series to show how each book links up with curriculum topics.

I am not going to cover all the topics covered by the National Curriculum as it would not only be lengthy, but largely irrelevant as far as, you, the children's writer is concerned. What new writers should remember is that educational publishers keep a close eye on curriculum developments and fashion their books accordingly. It is, therefore, no good coming up with some wildly fantastical – albeit possibly original – educational concept and expect educational publishers to fall over themselves to publish it. If it doesn't fit in with the requirements of the educational system then there isn't going to be a market for it. It's as simple as that.

WHAT IS THE LITERACY HOUR?

This is exactly as it sounds – an hour for teaching literacy skills. The definitions of this 'hour' were laid down in the National Literacy Strategy in the Framework for Teaching, and from September 1998 all primary schools have been expected to incorporate this literacy hour into the school day.

The hour is split into four distinct sections. The idea is that objectives are clearly explained and children are given frequent opportunities to review what they have learned. Explaining to others is a key ingredient of these sessions, as research has proven that this is one of the most effective methods of understanding and retaining information.

As the Literacy Hour progresses, children will learn to discriminate between separate sounds in words, read words by sounding out and blending their separate parts and write words by combining the spelling patterns of their sounds. Only in the latter stages, when children are reasonably fluent readers, will the emphasis shift to more advanced reading.

An understanding of the workings of the Literacy Hour is particularly important for writers wishing to write for Reading Schemes.

WHAT ARE PHONICS?

In the simplest educational terms, this is a method of teaching beginning readers to read and pronounce words by learning the sound of letters, letter groups and syllables. Sounds simple enough, but with reading standards falling and figures of adult illiteracy higher than ever, the argument continues to rage as to what is the best method to teach children to read.

A recent government-backed report, *The Rose Review of the Early Teaching of Reading,* is likely to have strong implications for children's educational publishers. The author of the report, Jim Rose, puts a strong case for the use of synthetic phonics in teaching children to read.

So how does it work? Synthetic phonics focus on sound. Children are taught the sound of letters pronounced in isolation and then blended. For example, they might break down the word 'cat' pronouncing each letter, and then blend the sounds back together again to form the word (I know, I know! To some of us this doesn't exactly sound revolutionary). They are also taught the sounds that combined letters make, for example 'oo' and 'ou'.

By contrast, using analytic phonics, instead of sounding aloud, involves teachers showing children how to deduce the common letter and sound among words that all begin (or end) with the same letter and sound. For example, pupils learning the letter and sound 'p', will discuss with their teacher how the words 'park', 'pat', 'pen' and 'push' are alike.

So what has all this got to do with me as a writer? you may well ask. Well, nothing in the short term. However, all writers, no matter what market they are writing for, should be aware of developing trends within children's books. Publishers such as Harcourt, Oxford University Press (OUP) and Ladybird are already leaping onto the synthetic phonics bandwagon, and, despite the 'say no to phonics before five' lobby, future reading schemes are likely to encompass at least some of Rose's recommendations. Authors, therefore, writing to specific 'briefs', which may well involve the use of synthetic phonics, need to understand what they are being asked to come up with.

What is a Reading Scheme?

You will be pleased to hear that Reading Schemes have made considerable progress since some of us were at school and most educational publishers today are producing lively, entertaining books with strong storylines. To achieve this, they use 'real' authors (i.e. authors who write for commercial/trade publishers as well) and are always on the lookout for talented new writers to add to their author lists.

Reading Schemes are books published by educational publishers for specific use in schools. Like Series Reads they conform to an easily identifiable look and length, but as far as writing them is concerned the approach is more akin to Series Fiction, in that the publisher provides the writer with a very detailed brief to work to.

Like Series Reads, the Reading Scheme market is open to new writers because it is the Scheme itself that is being promoted, not the author's name. However, it is a discipline with rigid rules, and this approach doesn't suit everyone.

There is one significant difference between the Series market and the Scheme market: educational publishers will not welcome material based on Schemes that they already publish. The educational market is a fast-moving one and publishers are always looking for new, original Schemes for a whole range of reading.

How to Write a Reading Scheme Book

It's best to make your initial approach to educational publishers by letter. State any relevant experience you may have – they will always be interested to hear from teachers, for example, who have first-hand experience of Reading Schemes – and send a sample of your writing. If your work seems suitable, you will be added to their list of authors and sent briefs of any appropriate future schemes.

These briefs can vary enormously. Some take up less than a side of A4, others go on for pages. This is one of the more simple variety, from Ginn (now part of www.myprimary.co.uk):

Reading 360 Pocket Books Levels 6, 7 and 8, Third Set
The Pocket Book series is a popular and successful range of illustrated paperbacks for newly independent readers. The books are grouped in Levels, which correspond to Levels 6 and 12 of Ginn's Reading 360 Scheme. These books are intended to be used as supplements to the main 360 Scheme and authors do not, therefore, have to worry about using a restricted vocabulary.

There are already eight books at each Level, and next year we are hoping to bring out a further set of four books at each of Levels 6, 7 and 8. Books in Level 6 are, on average, between 1500 and 2000 words long, and Level 8 books are usually between 2300 and 2500 words long.

Level 6 books are intended to appeal to children aged about six, and should be fairly simple in terms of plot and language level. Levels 7 and 8 are aimed at seven- and eight-year-olds, and can be slightly more complex, although simple, easily readable language and good, exciting plots are essential. We are looking for stories on a wide range of subjects, including family and friends, school, adventure, animals, dinosaurs, magic (though probably not ghosts or witches), sports, confronting fears, and fantasy. Stories with a multicultural background are particularly welcome.

You will note that this particular brief stresses that there is to be no use of 'restricted vocabulary'. However, a structured use of vocabulary is very important in many Reading Schemes, with specified words being carefully added to each level, building gradually on vocabulary used in the previous level.

As the notion of synthetic phonics gathers momentum, it goes without saying that author briefs will include the use of words following the 'phonic' format with the structure of words becoming more complicated as the reading levels progress, in order to cover the 40+ phonemes of the English language.

The educational market is a hard one to satisfy. Once

publishers have put together the framework of a Reading Scheme, it is 'trialled' in schools across the country, and there are no sterner critics than children themselves. For this reason, any writer wanting to contribute to this demanding genre should be aware of current teaching methods in primary schools. If you are not in day-to-day contact with young children (or even if you are), offer your services to your local primary school. Most primary schools have too many pupils and too few teachers, and will be only too happy to receive offers of voluntary help. As a writer, you can either read your work to selected classes, or, more usefully, hear children read. When a teacher has a class of thirty or more children of very mixed ability it is a godsend when someone is prepared to take a few of those children out of the classroom to give them individual help. It goes without saying, though, that if you are not known to the primary school concerned you should first make a formal approach to the Head Teacher in writing, stating exactly what you are offering and why.

Once you are working within the school system, you will soon realise (unless you live in a very remote rural area) that the children in each class are from a wide variety of social and ethnic backgrounds. For this reason, Reading Scheme texts are scrutinised intensely for political correctness. If you want to write for this market, you should be aware of this scrutiny and bear with it. For example, pigs may be loveable creatures – but Reading Schemes are destined for distribution throughout the entire country, including areas where large Moslem communities reside. Pigs are, for Moslems, taboo, and should therefore be avoided in Reading Scheme plots. Otherwise, publishers not only risk causing major offence but may also alienate themselves from a large sector of the buying market.

Reading Scheme: Exercise
Write a short story for children who are just beginning to read (5–6-year-olds) using the restricted word list below.

Points to remember:
- Stories should be between 300–400 words.
- Stories should be simple, with a beginning, a middle and an end. Choose a subject that children of this age and experience

will be interested in: starting school, dragons, animals, teddy bears, family life, dinosaurs etc.

- Set the story out on sixteen pages with Page 1 as the title page. Try to divide up the words fairly equally between pages.
- Keep sentences short and avoid sub-clauses. Each sentence should be no more than eight or nine words long, and there should be no more than six lines of text per page.
- Do not use indirect speech: John said he would go. Instead use direct speech: 'I will go,' said John.
- You may add to the word list by using characters' names (keep them simple) and any proper nouns that can be illustrated with a picture, so that if the reader does not know the word, he or she will be able to guess it from the illustration.

a	can't	gave	home	make
over	take	was	all	come
get	I	me	play	thank
we	am	could	give	if
must	put	that	went	an
cross	go	in	my	ran
the	were	and	day	going
into	no	run	them	what
as	did	good	is	not
sad	then	when	are	do
got	it	now	said	there
where	ask	don't	had	jumped
off	saw	they	who	at
down	happy	just	of	see
this	why	big	eat	have
laugh	old	she	to	will
blew	fell	he	laughed	on
sleep	too	wish	but	find
help	let's	one	so	tried
with	by	flew	her	little
open	some	under	would	called
fly	here	like	or	something
up	yes	came	for	him
looked	our	stop	very	you
can	from	his	made	out
swim	want	your		

GENERAL EDUCATIONAL FICTION

If, having read the above, you have decided that Reading Schemes are not for you then don't despair! There is still plenty of scope to write for the educational market even if you feel that phonics and use of a structured vocabulary would place too many constrictions on your creative 'flow'.

As well as Reading Schemes, schools need books to support and enhance the compulsory topics that are required to be taught during the course of a teaching day. This is especially the case bearing in mind the dictates of the National Curriculum and the Literacy Hour.

Children's author, Mal Leicester, has based her writing career to date on just such a premise and has several published books under her belt. Her earliest works broke new ground offering, for the first time, positive images of ethnic minority groups in children's books. Since then she has published three volumes of stories (with RoutledgeFalmer) for use in schools, dealing with a range of controversial topics such as bullying, prejudice and alternative lifestyles. Her most recent book, *Speical Stories for Disability Awareness* (Jessica Kingsley) breaks new ground yet again and is set to become widely used in the schools' market.

There is a huge range of topics open to authors when writing 'support' fiction. As well as the types of subjects mentioned above, there are less obvious areas that require discussion, especially when teaching Key Stages 1 and 2. Topics as general as 'promoting children's self-confidence' or 'developing their interpersonal skills' seem obvious to us as educated adults, yet for the child they are vital skills to be learned and honed.

Bear in mind that when handling sensitive topics such as these it is important to be subtle and gentle in your approach rather than direct and confrontational. For example, one of Mal's stories, *The Day the Sky Fell Down,* deals with 'kindness and compassion'. She writes a charming story of Beady, a young blackbird, who becomes lost and confused. He is rescued by Mr and Mrs Owl and, eventually, returned to his mum.

Interestingly, Madonna's *The English Roses* deals with much the same theme but in a more direct format. There is nothing wrong with this. Madonna's book is more commercial and targeted at the retail market. Mal's book is packaged completely differently. The story itself is targeted at very young children, yet the package as a whole is designed to be used by teachers. It consists of the story itself, but it also offers a lesson plan, a guide to vocabulary, discussion points and learning activities.

The discussion points include:
- How we feel when someone is kind to us and why we should be kind to others – even when we don't always want to be.
- Why we should be kind to animals.
- What we should do if we get lost.

The activity includes:
- Labelling the parts of a photocopied bird image – e.g. crown, beak, wings etc.
- Recognising birds.
- A practical activity; feeding birds.

Charities and Other Outlets

Occasionally, charities, and similar organisations, may be interested in financing the publication of stories that explain, or support, their particular cause. A few years ago, AceBabes (a national support group for parents of children born after fertility treatment) approached children's author, Mal Leicester, to help parents who have had fertility treatment to tell their children how they were conceived.

The brief was demanding. AceBabes wanted a story, not an information book. They wanted to target the book at very young children, yet they still wanted the story to go some way towards explaining what *in vitro* fertilisation (IVF) is all about. For young children, the subject of conception is hard enough to understand – one would think that explaining IVF would be almost impossible!

However, Mal persevered and the resulting book, *Making Miracles*, sees Ferdy the Frog enlist the help of a boy called Adam to find his missing frog spawn to make sure the baby frogs are born in springtime. Adam later discovers he was born as a result of assisted conception. He learns how doctors helped his mother have a baby in a similar way to the help he gave Ferdy.

The fact that it was possible to create a sympathetic children's information book from what could be conceived as purely scientific subject matter, was of great benefit to AceBabes and the small storybook has formed a valuable backbone to future publicity campaigns.

As Mal herself said, 'We are aware that there are other, more technical, books around, but our aim is to provide a story, and a character, that can touch on the subject and be an opening.'

Putting Educational Ideas into Practise

If you have a good idea, and feel that there is a market for it, you need to consider how you are going to approach your potential publisher or backer. This is a completely different ballgame to targeting educational reading schemes as you are, to all intents and purposes, proposing a new, uncharted idea.

So consider the following points:
- What is your book about?
- What are its main themes and objectives?
- Why is your book different to, or better than, any other similar book on the market?
- Who is your book aimed at? Who will buy it? Who will read it?
- And, most importantly: Why are you, as opposed to anyone else, qualified to write it?

Lastly, you must be prepared to back your proposal up with one or two sample chapters or, in the cases of very short stories, a complete manuscript.

Educational Fiction: Exercise
- Write a short story for 5–6-year-olds of between 500–1000 words promoting respect for world religions.
- Provide three related discussion points based on the story.
- Come up with an 'activity' related to the story.

CHAPTER FOUR

GENERAL FICTION FOR 8–12-YEAR-OLDS

The mechanics of reading have (hopefully) been mastered by the time a child is eight or nine; they can then venture into the big, wide world of independent reading.

Books for this age group are considerably longer than those in the Young Fiction category. They also tend to be published not in series, but as stand-alone titles – just as are the majority of books for adults. However, as there are a few Series Reads around for 8–12-year-olds, I will deal with these as well at the end of this chapter.

Times have changed and, in my opinion, this is probably the best area of any publisher's list to target if you are a new, unpublished writer. Publishers are constantly on the lookout for good, strong stories for both boys and girls and, as in teenage fiction, the individual editor's tastes will play a significant part in the publishing decision, i.e. they want to take on books that they, personally, like and would buy.

Beware, though, if you have been working on that 'magnum opus' for most of your life and feel that, at last, there is now a marketplace for it! Even if an editor thinks your book is the best submission she has ever seen, she will not be interested in taking it on if it is the one and only thing you have ever written, and are ever likely to write. In other words, both editorial and sales/marketing departments need to feel confident that they are taking on a new author who will go on to write many further books for their lists.

Convincing a publisher that you wish to make a 'career' out of writing children's books is now important for all sectors of the marketplace, but I would say that it is *most* important when writing General Fiction. Children's fiction is, at last, starting to catch up with the adult sector and it is now possible to earn huge advances when writing stand-alone novels. Indeed, if a manuscript is good enough, it is not unusual to have several publishers all pitching for the same title. But, in many ways, they are not pitching for the title alone but for the privilege of having you, the author, as part of their 'team'. And they will only want to do this if they feel you show real potential and promise as a Writer with a capital 'W'.

This is worth bearing in mind should you be lucky enough to be invited to discuss your submission with an editor, as likeability (yours not theirs) is going to play a factor in whether or not the editor will want to take your work any further. If you come across as difficult, inflexible and demanding, they will think twice about making you an offer even if your manuscript is brilliant. However, if you take the time to empathise with the editor and show them that you are approachable and open to ideas, they are far more likely to consider you as a serious contender. It's a bit like going for a job interview in a way, so familiarising yourself with that publisher's list won't do any harm either.

Okay, over with the lecture and on with the facts.

What to Write About?

The fun part about writing for 8–12-year-olds is that you can write about almost anything. The serious, the funny, the outrageous and the downright controversial will all be considered if centred around a strong, original and relevant theme.

I'm going to talk more about specific subject matter areas in Chapter Ten of this book. In this chapter, I want to talk about the decision-making process that comes into play before you even put pen to paper – or fingers to keyboard.

Inexperienced writers, in my opinion, fall into two categories; they are either spilling over with ideas but have given no thought at all to the age group they are going to target; or they are more circumspect, have studied the market in detail and are struggling to come up with an idea that, either, a) is fashionable or b) has never been done before.

If you are in the first category – i.e. spilling over with ideas – then listen up. I know I said you could write about almost anything, but I didn't mean it. Well, I did, but with the emphasis on 'almost'. A 25,000-word story about the tooth fairy simply isn't going to interest a 12-year-old child – I don't care how edgy the tooth fairy is! It may, however, interest a 5-year-old but they will have neither the ability, nor the stamina, to wade through a book of this length.

If you are in the second group – i.e. market aware but searching around for good ideas – then stop looking at the market and stop agonising over ideas. The best writers for this age group write for themselves. So think about what you want to do with your writing – either why you want to write for this age group or what you would like to read about if you were still between the ages of 8 and 12. Here's Philip Ridley's take on the subject:

> I'm increasingly concerned to help children confront their problems. My stories are obsessed with all the modern sources of anxiety: with money, poverty, vanity, ageing, decay, but I want to express these anxieties in a way that cuts through all that stuff to the core of what really matters, which is, I suppose, a kind of solidarity in adversity. In *Krindlekrax* it's Ruskin's love for his friend the school-keeper that causes him to confront the dragon, and in doing so to heal a whole street. *Meteorite Spoon* is almost entirely about violent argument and disappointment, but in the end the children teach their parents the value of love. If I had to sum up what I'm trying to do in my books, I'd say it's an attempt to make children feel less lonely in their fears.

Of course, there is, also, a third group of writers – those who think that their best chance of publishing success is to emulate the bestsellers: that they either have to write an adventure story in the style of Enid Blyton, or a funny book in the style of Roald

Dahl. Both writers wrote wonderful and extremely popular books – but they are unique, and any imitation is a waste of time. *Be original.* Not only because imitations are easy to spot, but because children's publishing is very innovative and creative and new ideas will find more favour than recycled old ones. When doing your reading research, be sure to read books by contemporary living authors as well as dead ones! Observe children you know in this age group – what do they like to read? What are their interests and hobbies?

When coming up with ideas for the 8–12 age group, it is important to keep your mind as open as possible. Never rule anything out on the grounds that it isn't 'suitable' or is 'too old'. Children in this age range are just starting to realise that life isn't as simple as they once thought and they are perfectly capable of handling 'grown-up' subjects so long as they are presented in an accessible way.

Take the following passage from *Goodnight Mister Tom* by Michelle Magorian:

> The small alcove stank of stale urine and vomit. A thin emaciated boy with matted hair and skin like parchment was tied to a length of copper piping. He held a small bundle in his arms. His scrawny limbs were covered with sores and bruises and he sat in his own excrement. He shrank at the light from the torch and made husky gagging noises. The warden reached out and touched him and he let out a frightened whimper. An empty baby's bottle stood by his legs.

The 'bundle' is, in fact, a dead baby. The boy is covered in sores and bruises because he has been violently abused by his own mother and left to die in wartime London during the Blitz. As you can see, this author doesn't shrink from tackling quite disturbing topics – one which would not be out of place in adult fiction.

This book is aimed at children of nine or ten years upwards, and deals with subjects that some adults might find shocking. However, it is very much a children's book because it tells the story of a nine-year-old boy entirely from the child's point-of-view. Exclusively adult aspects of this book, such as the boy's mother's suicide, are is dealt with simplistically. The style renders the subject matter palatable, and softens any sharp edges.

In other words, it doesn't matter if your novel's characters get hurt or suffer in some way. The important thing is that the major players have to change and develop in a *positive* way. At the end of the book, there has to be a feeling of hope, a feeling of: 'Here I am. This is my name.'

Having said that, it is important to remember when writing for this age group – particularly if creating stories based on the more gruelling aspects of life – that a completely downbeat narrative with no highspots or humour will not be acceptable. Just as editors don't fill their newspapers with only bad news (because no one would buy them!), successful authors don't fill children's books with nothing but negativity.

Finally, on this subject of 'what to write about', after years of attempting to publish 'unisex' books, publishers are waking up to the fact that boys and girls have very different interests – particularly between the ages of eight and twelve. A few years ago, writers and publishers alike struggled to create books that would appeal to both sexes, often resulting in anodyne covers and weak characterisation. Of course, the more literate child will read everything and anything that is going. However, publishers soon realised that they needed to work harder to win over the more reluctant readers – especially boys – and produce books that specifically 'pushed their buttons'.

So, today, as a writer, it is possible to embrace the gender gap rather than try to fill it. There are writers such as Cathy Cassidy writing specifically for girls, and there are writers such as Charlie Higson writing specifically for boys. So if you have an idea but are worried that, perhaps, it won't bridge the gender gap, then this should no longer be grounds for huge concern. If your main character is a girl, then don't feel compelled to stick a boy in as her best friend just so that boys will be interested in your story too. Similarly, if your book is an all-action, boys' own adventure, then don't struggle to introduce female sidekicks. Such artificial manipulation of plots will only get in the way of what could be a great story for girls, and only girls, or boys, and only boys.

Of course, there are plenty of writers writing very successfully for both sexes – Eoin Colfer, J. K. Rowling, Malorie Blackman etc. – and that's great too.

How Long?

Too long, in my opinion, is anything over 40,000 words. Too short is anything under 20,000 words. Everything in between is fine.

The 40,000-word novel is, of necessity, going to need a higher cover price – which, in turn, will make it harder to sell. The novel of less than 20,000 words is better targeted at the Reading Series market.

So what does 20,000 or 40,000 words actually look like? Let's take a couple of well-known titles. *Goodnight Mister Tom* by Michelle Magorian is well over 40,000 words; *Matilda* by Roald Dahl is around 20,000 words.

You can argue this question of a 'right' length until the cows come home. And, believe me, some authors do!

'But my book's as long as it's long.'
'My text dictates its length to me, not the other way round.'
'But I couldn't possibly cut it. It's all far too good!'

These are some of the comments levelled at me as an editor when I dare to suggest that a submission is being turned down purely on grounds of its length. After all, some of the Harry Potter books weigh in at two or three times my specified maximum length of 40,000 words – and we all know how successful they've been!

It is true that publishers are now more willing than they were to take on longer texts, particularly in the fantasy sector. However, I would still suggest that new writers don't go shorter than 20,000. It's all about giving yourself the 'best possible chance' of being published and that's not going to happen if you veer too far wide of the accepted marking points in terms of length.

SERIES READS FOR 8–12-YEAR-OLDS

Some children, particularly if they have had difficulty in coming to terms with reading, find the General Fiction market intimidating. For them, the array of books is vast and confusing and they have no idea if, having chosen a book, they will be capable of finishing it. On the other hand, they don't want to stay reading 'baby' books either.

For this very particular area of the market, some publishers have increased their Series Read range to encompass much longer books. They are targeted at children of eight upwards but still offer the more reluctant reader the security of knowing exactly what they are buying in terms of interest level and length.

This is a relatively small market and not one that I would necessarily suggest targeting, but, for reference, have included a chart of titles.

Series Title	Word Count	Age Level	Publisher
Black Cats	9000–14,000 words	7–10	A & C Black
Flashbacks	12,000–14,000 words	8 +	A & C Black
Red Apples	20,000–25,000 words	9–12	Orchard Books
Bite	35,000+ words	12 +	Hodder Children's Books
Black Apples	30,000–40,000 words	12 +	Orchard Books

Stand-Alone Fiction: Exercises

- Consider the different subject matters that are on offer for this age group and establish which area you think you might be most qualified to write about.
- Pay a visit to your local children's library or bookshop and browse through as many titles (contemporary authors, as well please!) as possible that handle your chosen subject matter.
- Think of your own idea for a Stand-Alone Fiction title.
- Write a one-page story outline, based on your idea (but do not plot it out in detail until you have read the chapters on 'Subject Matter' and 'Plotting' in Part II).

CHAPTER FIVE

TEENAGE
FICTION

A few years ago, publishers' trade magazine the *Bookseller* asked its readers, when is a teenage book not a teenage book? Answer, when it looks like being so successful that adult lists want it too.

Which pretty well sums up the problems involved in trying to create a book specifically targeted at teenagers. Teenagers – *real* teenagers – (i.e. children of thirteen-plus) don't read Teenage Fiction, they read adult books. This makes the term teenager a bit of a misnomer. Many publishers/librarians/booksellers have tried to circumnavigate this problem by re-naming this publishing category Young Adult Fiction. Nonetheless, despite this attempt to give Teenage Fiction wider appeal, all children's publishers recognise that teenage books are in fact read and enjoyed by children as young as ten.

If you don't believe me, go and spend some time in your local children's library during term-time. Third- and fourth-year juniors will pounce on the teenage shelves with enthusiasm. However, children at secondary level won't be seen dead in the children's section. These older children are more likely to be in the adult library, acting cool, plucking reading material from under the noses of more senior readers.

There is one argument that suggests that there should be no formal separation between teenage reading and adult reading: that books specifically targeted at the teenager are a fairly recent phenomenon imported from America. However, (as all you aspiring teenage writers will be glad to hear!) there is a market for Teenage Fiction, albeit fairly small.

Teenage Fiction is aimed at children in the age range of approximately 11–16 – a very wide band. These years can be fraught with turbulent emotion and insecurities and Teenage Fiction can help young people explore often very disturbing feelings in a safe and un-embarrassing way. It is performing a social function: acting as a reassuring, sympathetic and wise best friend.

WHAT TO WRITE ABOUT?

It is true that Teenage Fiction can help young people explore their emotions but don't be under the allusion that all Teenage Fiction should, therefore, be issue-based. In fact, according to Chris and Tim Cross, the brothers who started www.cool-reads.co.uk (a website devoted to teenagers reviewing Teenage Fiction), a lot of teenagers are very wary of 'issuey' books.

Another common misconception about Teenage Fiction is that all teen books have to be gritty and contemporary – such as Melvyn Burgess's *Junk*. Teenagers, like adults, have a wide variety of tastes and what we, as authors, choose to write about should reflect this.

According to a survey conducted by the Cool-Reads website, there are three important factors that dictate how teenagers select the books that they read. These are 1) the topic itself (i.e. what the book is about), 2) whether or not it is by an author they like and 3) whether or not the book cover impresses them.

As new writers, there is nothing you can do about the second factor because, obviously, you haven't had anything published yet so no one knows whether they like your books or not – yet! There is also no point in giving any thought to the cover before you've even started writing the words. So the one, single, most important factor that remains is 'topic', or subject matter. What you choose to write about is going to hugely influence whether or not your teenage book makes it onto the shelves and, once there, whether anyone buys it.

Cool-Reads divide their review categories into fourteen general topic areas.

Mystery and adventure
Suspense and horror
Action stories
Survival
Animal and nature
Real life
War
Romance and love stories
Characters and school stories
People/Places/In the past
Fun stuff
Biography
Short stories and snappy reads
Sports

Obviously, each of these categories can be split into sub-categories, and most titles fall into more than one category, but the very fact that there is such a large selection of topic areas to choose from shows just how varied the teenage diet can be. Basically, there are no set topics from which to choose as far as writing for teenagers is concerned. You can write about anything and everything, and people do.

Write about what excites *you* and not what you think will excite your audience. Because our teen years was the last phase of our childhood before we became grown-ups – at twenty (as if!), most of us can remember what if felt like to be a teenager (probably because most of us carry on feeling exactly the same for years and years). So if you write about something that interests *you*, that excites *you*, then the likelihood is it will interest and excite someone else as well.

When asked what her favourite teenage book was, writer Louise Rennison replied: 'I don't read teenage books because I am not a teenager. In truth I really am very ignorant about the whole "teen" thing and that's how I want it to stay. I deliberately don't read anyone else's books. I just plug into what I remember about my own teen times.'

Reader, please do not ignore current teen fiction. However, I get her point.

Don't, for a minute, feel ashamed should you want to write

something that might not be considered 'quality' or educational. I was recently telephoned by Disgusted of Tunbridge Wells. She had read an article in a Sunday newspaper that stated that it didn't matter if children read bus tickets, so long as they were reading. She objected to this attitude and wanted to quote me in her letter of reply to the newspaper, denigrating what she described as 'rubbish'. Needless to say, I refused to do so.

Let teenagers read bus tickets if they want to: let them read pop magazines, let them read escapist rubbish, or hopefully, the classics – but for goodness' sake, don't take away their freedom of choice. It's a question of 'horses for courses' – and as you know, you can lead a horse to water but you can't make him drink. Teenagers aren't inclined to be forced into activities against their will; reading a book of any description, no matter how 'rubbishy' by adult standards, is surely better than being stimulated by nothing other than the latest computer game. All written material engenders an affection for, and understanding of, words and how they can be used to best effect. And the wider the variety of books teenagers want to read, the more opportunities that exist for the new writer!

HOW TO BE COOL

Having decided what to write about, the next big hurdle is how to write in a way that will actually appeal to teenagers. How do you talk their talk, dream their dreams, tap into their world and mentality? In other words, how do you write to be cool?

The simple answer is that you don't. Indeed, children's author, Adèle Geras, believes that writers should forget about their audience altogether, and write entirely to please themselves. She says: 'The less-than-good teenage books happen, I think, when a writer sits down and says to herself, "I'm going to write a book that'll go down a bomb with all the groovy dudes down at the disco." That's writing a book *de haut en bas*, and it shows. Always.'

I do believe, however, that in order to write successfully for teenagers, you do need to *like* teenagers and have some understanding as to where they are coming from. I'm not talking about hanging around your local youth club, but if you wholly disapprove of texting and having conversations on the Internet, if you, like, don't get the way they, like, speak or perhaps you do get it – not, and still think that words like bare (very), long (person: annoying/distance: far), gay (sad) and fat[1] mean, well, bare, long, gay and fat (don't ask!) then perhaps this isn't the market for you.

I'm not suggesting that you use said trendy vocabulary – in fact, definitely don't as it will immediately date your book. For example, I've just asked my teenage daughter, for purposes of research for this chapter, to give me some of the funny words she uses with translations. When she said, what funny words, I said words like 'fat'. At which point she looked at me as though I'd been drinking and said that I was SOOOO sad, NO ONE uses 'fat' any more and I'd never really got what it meant in the first place. She also said I'd better run this chapter past her before publication because otherwise I was bound to get it 'hideously wrong'. So there you go.

All I'm trying to say is that in order to write for teenagers you need to understand that they are exactly the same as adults but with an important difference – they don't *think* they're the same. In fact, they think they're unique and different and special, and that they invented their world and that everyone else is ancient and that no one understands them, and . . . and that's okay. That's how they are, that's why we love them and that's why we want to write great books for them.

VIEWPOINT

What sets Teenage Fiction apart from Adult Fiction is that all books specifically targeted at the teen market feature a teenage character and the story is usually told through teenage eyes. It would also be true to say that most adult books enjoyed by teenagers also feature a young adult character as part of the story even if they aren't necessarily in their teen years – for example,

---

[1] Following advice from my daughter, 'fat' turned out to be spelled 'phat', which, apparently, dates back to the '80s and '90s and is an acronym for 'Pretty Hips And Thighs' – although others have speculated that it was drawn from 'physically attractive'.

A Long Way Down by Nick Hornby, *I Capture the Castle* by Dodi Smith and *The Lost Art of Keeping Secrets* by Eva Rice.

This question of viewpoint can lead to another criticism of Teenage Fiction that sometimes, particularly when writing about serious subjects, the negative side of life is glossed over in favour of the positive.

Berlie Doherty's *Dear Nobody*, the story of an unplanned teenage pregnancy, won the Carnegie Medal and is generally accepted as being a fine piece of writing. However, it has its critics, who find it disturbing that young schoolgirls should be encouraged to regard it as acceptable to become parents. The book does end on rather a positive note, given the gravity of the situation, and any concerns over the future of either baby or Mum remain unarticulated. Says Helen, the young mother, after her baby is born: 'A baby isn't the end of everything. It's the beginning of something else.'

Contrast that with Margaret Drabble's *adult* book on illegitimate birth, *The Millstone*, where the baby is born halfway through the action, leaving the narrator plenty of time to conclude that, 'It was a bad investment.'

My own feelings as an editor are that Teenage Fiction is most successful when it strikes a balance. Teenagers don't want to listen to moral lectures – they want to find out what's right and wrong for themselves, and they aren't going to read/buy books that are too 'preachy' and seem to dictate a code of behaviour. On the other hand, they want a healthy dose of realism in their reading; they're starting to live in the adult world, and they don't want writers to show them a version of reality in which unpleasant truths are examined through rose-tinted spectacles. It's perfectly possible to convey a serious message in a positive way.

LENGTH

Many writers feel that, because it is written for an older market, Teenage Fiction must be much longer than a book for the under-12s. In fact, nothing could be further from the case. A book that is too hefty will entail a high cover price, which will take it well outside the normal children's market price range. Not a good idea as far as sales are concerned. At this age, a young person is likely to be becoming more independent financially and, as far as spending money is concerned, they are spoiled for choice. The humble book is competing with cosmetics, clothes, gadgets, booze, fags and just having a good time. The price, therefore, needs to be attractive.

I would say it is rare for a publisher to take on Teenage Fiction over 50,000 words. Too short a book, however, is often viewed as insubstantial, not offering enough of a challenge or value for money. My advice to a new writer working on a teenage novel would be to aim at a word count of around 30–40,000 words. This is to give yourself **the best possible chance of being published**. There are, of course, exceptions to every rule.

THE CROSSOVER BOOK

Although it is perceived as a recent phenomenon (started by the first Harry Potter book) the 'crossover' book has, in fact, been around for a long time.

In the first edition of this book, I wrote about a book called *Sophie's World* by Jostein Gaarder. This was first published as a teenage book in Norway but was then picked up by a British publisher and placed firmly on their adult list. However, since the *Harry Potter* series proved that children's books can cut across generations, and be enjoyed by adults just as much as by children, the whole concept of the 'crossover' book has picked up pace.

I am not talking, here, about adult books that also appeal to teenagers – such as the titles mentioned earlier – but a very specific drive to push children's books into the adult arena. Mark Haddon's *The Curious Incident of the Dog in the Night-time* proved that a children's book can become an adult bestseller. This particular book was helped along with two different cover looks – one for children and one for adults – and similar marketing strategies have been used for other children's titles. *A Gathering Light* by Jennifer Donelly, *The Boy in the Striped Pyjamas* by John Boyne and *Across the Nightingale Floor* by Lian Hearn, are just a few examples of books that have done better as adult editions than in their original children's incarnations.

If a publisher is lucky, a book will pick up an adult audience without the help of dual additions. For example, Meg Rossoff's wonderful *How I Live Now* deservedly picked up the Branford Boase Award and the Guardian Children's Fiction Prize as well as being short-listed for the Orange new writers' award.

This crossover market is one worth knowing about from the new writer's point-of-view. I'm not suggesting that you sit down and think 'I'm going to write a crossover book', but if you do write a book that is likely to appeal to a wide audience it is going to appeal to your potential publisher as well. In terms of how books are sold, crossover marketing and dual editions are a way of getting really wonderful stories into as many people's hands as possible.

Recent years have seen a redefining of content as far as books for older children and teenagers are concerned. Adult publishers are waking up to the fact that children's publishers are bringing out fantastically well-told stories and that they are becoming ever more sophisticated. Past limitations, particularly in the areas of sex and violence, have become blurred and this exciting area of the book world offers greater opportunities to the new writer than ever before.

Teenage Fiction: Exercises

- Select an adult book that you like that features a teenage character at some point in the story.
- Taking that character, think about how you could write a completely different story from their perspective. It doesn't matter how far you stray from the original plot.
- Start writing the first few paragraphs of the book trying to establish an upbeat, pacey, readable writing style. Write from the teenager's viewpoint but write for yourself as well.

CHAPTER SIX

THE SHORT STORY

SHORT STORIES

Not so long ago, I ran a one-day seminar 'Writing Children's Books and Short Stories'. It quickly became apparent that many new writers are not aware of any difference between the two: a children's book is short; a children's short story is more of the same, but possibly shorter still.

The most obvious shortcoming of this argument is that not everything written for children is short. Novels for older children are, by adult standards, short, but at 20,000 words or more they can in no way be described as a short story. Books for younger children are short but, as I firmly told one delegate at the seminar, there is a huge difference between writing a short children's *book* and writing a short story.

'Really?' she queried. 'What?'

At which point I was stopped in my tracks. What exactly *is* the difference between, for example, a 300-word Reader and a 3000-word short story?

Chapters for one thing. Most 3000-word books have chapters, breaking the story up into episodes, whereas a 3000-word short story is a continuous piece of text.

The late Nancy Smith described writing the short story as being rather like 'taking a day trip somewhere, when there is no time to deviate from your destination. The novel, on the other hand, is more akin to a fortnight's holiday during which you can wander off the main route to admire the scenery, visit other places of interest, if you so desire.'

Nancy was talking about adult writing; I'm not absolutely sure that, when writing for children, there is ever much time to deviate from the main path. However, she has a point: a children's short story has to get to the point in one episode, whereas a children's short book has more scope.

Dick King-Smith's short book *Clever Duck* is about a bright young duck named Damaris who teams up with her sheepdog friend, Rory, to rid the farmyard of the pigs who have plagued their lives for so long. The story takes place over a period of time. Chapter Three opens: 'Now in summer-time some months later . . .'

This time span would not be possible in a children's short story, which, as a general rule, takes place during a very short period of time. To quote Nancy Smith again: 'The short story is always concerned with a small but significant incident in the life of the main character.'

So in a short *story* by Dick King-Smith – very much the same sort of length as *Clever Duck* – 'The Rats of Meadowsweet Farm' (from the short-story anthology *Muck and Magic: Stories from the Countryside*), the author deals with the rats' revenge on Farmer Green for massacring thirty of their population. Unlike *Clever Duck*, this story takes place over a single night.

Obviously, a certain amount of background information will need to be included in any short story to explain, and set up, the plot. This is usually best done using little anecdotes interspersed within the main text.

For example, take the opening of the following story:

'Closed or closed?' said Mum, standing by the little window in Katie's attic bedroom, one hand on the rusty latch.

'Closed,' mumbled Katie, sinking down under her duvet so that only her eyes peeped out over the top.

Mum laughed and let the curtains drop back. She'd asked the same question every night since they'd moved. She thought it was funny. Katie didn't. She didn't think it was funny at all.

'Perhaps Dad'll have time to fix it this weekend,' said Mum, still smiling.

Katie shook her head and sank down a little further. She didn't want Dad to fix it. Not this weekend. Not ever.

From this we learn that Katie has moved house and that, for some reason yet to be discovered, Katie is frightened of something outside her new home and doesn't want her window opened under any circumstances. All the relevant background detail has been filled in without holding up the main body of the story.

Markets

Having tried to define the short story, I am now going to be very irritating and tell you that the market for children's short stories is very small.

Short-story collections by one author are hard to sell unless the author is already well known. For this reason, children's publishers are reluctant to take on this type of book from new writers. However, it has been known. Malorie Blackman was a new writer when she had her collection of teenage short stories, *Not So Stupid!*, accepted by Women's Press for their Livewire series. But be warned – you face an uphill struggle.

If you are intent on trying to get a collection of short stories accepted, I would suggest giving them some sort of 'theme'. The stories in *Not So Stupid!* all feature girls who are, in some way, fighting back at society.

Short-story collections about one *character* will probably stand a better chance of success than a random collection on a particular subject. This is especially true when writing for the Young Fiction market.

While scouring the bookshelves of your local children's bookshop or library, you will notice that even short-story anthologies (i.e. a collection of stories by a number of different authors) are almost always themed in some way. Kingfisher publish a wide selection of themed short-story anthologies. For example, their *Treasury of …* series features pony, pet, dragon and ballet stories in four separate collections.

A short-story anthology will still feature one name on the

cover – that of the editor. Editors chosen for this task are some-times high-profile names, with their name being the main marketing tool used to sell the book. Other times an editor could simply be the in-house editor working on the book.

Wendy Cooling, Chris Powling, Pat Thompson and Tony Bradman are all well-known editorial names in the short-story anthology genre. If you don't have an agent, I would suggest getting in touch with the editors direct, via their publishers. They may then include you on their mailing lists and send you details of anthologies in preparation. I know several authors who have successfully placed work in this way.

MAGAZINE SHORT STORIES

Twenty years ago, writers were spoiled for choice when it came to placing short stories in children's comics and magazines. Publishing houses such as IPC and DC Thomson were falling over each other in the mad rush to publish titles for children and teenagers. Remember *Tammy*, *Mandy*, *Bunty*, *Blue Jeans*, *Jackie*, *Oh Boy!*, *My Guy*, *Photo-Love*, *Photo Secret Love*, *Girl*, *She*, *Hers*, *Loving* . . .? The list went on and on.

Today, however, the picture is rather bleaker. There are still plenty of magazines out there, together with a handful of comics, but the opportunities they present are very different. Magazines such as *Jackie* and *My Guy* have long since been replaced by weekly and monthly publications featuring articles on lifestyle topics and the music world, with the occasional piece of fiction thrown in for light relief.

If you're determined to write stories for the magazine market, go into a large newsagents' and have a good, long browse. Buy any titles that interest you and get a feel for the sort of profile they are trying to achieve. Most importantly, read the fiction, making a careful note of word counts and subject matter. There's no earthly point in writing a 3000-word story about a marital affair if all the readers are fourteen or under and the magazine has no more than 3000 words in total!

It's helpful to contact the magazines you have chosen to target in writing or by phone and see if they issue editorial guidelines. Many magazines are more than happy to receive such requests, as they are keen to avoid having to wade through piles of unsuitable material. Guidelines generally give you a reader profile (male or female, age, whether they're studying or working, what type of reading material he/she might favour etc.) and then go on to specify what they are looking for in terms of a publishable story (number of characters, amount of dialogue, themes and so on).

Stories with some kind of twist are popular with many magazines. One I wrote very early on in my writing career (for *Loving* magazine) told the story of a judo fight – the twist was that the two fighting were girlfriend and boyfriend . . . 'Tricking' the reader into thinking that a couple don't know each other when they do is a well-worn concept and you will see it repeated again and again. It doesn't matter how often you repeat a theme, so long as you give it a sufficiently different angle each time, ensuring that the 'twist' continues to surprise. And no matter whether your short story has a 'twist in the tale' or not, the reader should never be able to guess the ending with complete certainty.

PHOTOSTORIES AND COMICS

Another fiction market that, like the magazine short story, has experienced a decline over the past fifteen years is the 'photostory' and 'picture-strip' market. Photostories are stories told in a series of photographs with accompanying speech bubbles; picture-strips are stories told in a series of drawn images with accompanying speech bubbles and/or text. Although still popular in mainland Europe, there are virtually no photostory magazines being published in this country any more.

One of the reasons for the decline of photostories is that they cost a lot of money to produce. As well as the writer, models and a photographer are required, not to mention location fees, costume charges and printing costs.

Picture-strips (comic-strips) are a little different because, as the writer, you don't have to worry about cost. Because the pictures to illustrate your story are drawn by an artist, there are no boundaries. Below are the first four frames from a photostory written for a *Photo-Love* annual. This is how the original manuscript looked. A comic-strip is written in much the same way except you need to bear in mind that your visual descriptions are for an illustrator and not a photographer, so you can let you imagination run riot. One word of warning though – check the nationality of the artist. When I was writing for the comic *Tammy,* all the artwork was done in Spain, where graphic styling is very different. The interpretation of my picture descriptions could sometimes be unusual to say the least!

Dangerous Image

1

Beth and Anna in a living room. Anna has just come into the room and is propping up a pair of skis against the wall. She looks sneeringly over at Beth. Beth is sitting down looking up at her defensively.

TOP PANEL: The tension has been growing for days …
ANNA: God, Beth – sitting around as usual! You're incredible …
BETH: Just shut up, Anna. I don't even know why I ever agreed to come on this skiing holiday with you …

2

Closing in on Beth and Anna. Anna is standing close to Beth now, hands on hips. Beth is getting angrier.

BETH: I really was fool enough to think we could get on!
ANNA: How can we get on when you obviously hate my guts?

3

Beth is looking away from Anna at point on floor. Shoot looking up at Beth from below so that Anna is standing behind her. Beth looks sad and bitter. Anna is raising her eyes to the ceiling in exasperation.

BETH: Well, are you surprised after what you did to me? You – my own twin sister!
ANNA: Oh, God, we're not going to go through all that again, are we?

4

Beth has leapt to her feet and is face on to Anna, shouting at her angrily. Anna looks taken aback.

BETH: Well, why shouldn't I go through it again? You've stolen the only man I've ever loved ...

ANNA: Oh, Beth, do you think I ever really wanted him?

Once the script is finished, the story is ready to shoot or, in the case of comic-strip, to go to an artist.

Over the past year, both *Jackie* and *My Guy* have been brought out as special edition Christmas annuals. I have had great fun looking at some of my old short stories and photostories, picking out now-famous faces from the photostory frames. This type of modelling work used to be very popular as a means of subsistence for up-and-coming actors: Tracey Ullman, for example, supplemented her income during her early career by doing photostories. As did Hugh Grant, George Michael and many other celebrites who, I'm sure, would rather remain name-less!

But like the actors and models, writers are not going to make their fortune from writing the children's short story. Compared to writing a short children's book, children's short-story writing does not pay well. Payment for short stories accepted for anthologies is usually made on a flat-fee basis and can rarely be described as generous. However, having a short story accepted often provides the first taste of publishing success for many writers. The short story can provide an excellent leg-up on to the first rung of the publishing ladder.

Short Story: Exercise

- Pay a visit to your local children's bookshop or library and select a short-story anthology. Imagine you have been asked to write a story for the anthology concerned and see what you come up with.
- Pay a visit to your local newsagent and select any magazine that contains short-story fiction. Contact the editorial depart-ment and ask if they produce editorial guidelines. Write a story sticking to those guidelines (if they don't provide guide-lines, follow the example of other stories in the magazine).

CHAPTER SEVEN

NON-FICTION

One of the most original and exciting submissions I have seen on a 'slush pile' arrived late one afternoon in a large cardboard suitcase. It was filled with twenty pairs of hand-made, paper shoes, which I and my colleagues spent an extremely enjoyable couple of hours examining, admiring and trying on.

The submission was entitled *The Paper Shoe Book*, by Chris Knowles and Julian Horsey. As well as the suitcase of shoes, the authors had supplied two dummy books – one targeted at children, one at adults. The books supplied everything the reader needed for making their own pair of paper shoes (except for pencil, felt-tips, scissors and glue).

Sadly, it wasn't right for our list. At our suggestion, however, the authors took their idea to a packager who, in turn, sold the book to Random House where it was published under their, then, specialist books imprint, Ebury Press.

I tell this story because it highlights a number of points that should be taken into account when trying to break into the children's non-fiction market, which, it should be said, often offers a readier route into publication than fiction. The natural curiosity of children, combined with a school curriculum that not only covers many subjects of interest but also includes non-fiction in the Literacy Hour, creates an enormous market

So what characterises good non-fiction for children?

Who Are You Writing For?

The first point to consider is what, exactly, your market consists of – i.e. who is your book for. However good a writer you are, publishers must be confident that there are sufficient readers out there who want to spend their money buying your book. Publishers are often unwilling to even look at books that are outside the range of books they normally publish.

The authors of *The Paper Shoe Book* certainly considered their market carefully but, by targeting their proposal at both adults *and* children, they aimed too wide. Eventually, this particular book was marketed as an adult novelty title, rather than a book for children.

As a non-fiction writer for children it is vital to understand your market – and I don't mean just taking on board that your book is for children rather than adults. Just like any other area of the children's market, non-fiction is divided into age ranges – titles suitable for the under-5's, titles for 6–8-year-olds, titles for age 9+ and titles for teens.

When writing children's non-fiction, you will need to provide enough information so that children can understand the concepts, without providing so much information that they become confused. The degree and type of information is clearly constrained by the envisaged age of your target readership, so it is important to have a clear understanding of the development of children's thinking. Broadly speaking, the younger the child, the simpler and more concrete the level of information needs to be.

Additional material suggesting activities for children to carry out, or reading lists enabling them to expand their understanding of the subject matter, are a good way of providing a link to more complex information for those who wish to pursue it, while keeping the text at an appropriate level for most readers of your target age.

Is it Different?

The Paper Shoe Book was certainly different. It isn't every day that a large suitcase of paper shoes lands on my desk! However, it isn't only the appearance of the proposal that has to be original and eye-catching. The author of children's non-fiction has to find unique ways of approaching familiar subjects by giving them new angles and new perspectives.

Never is this more true than when writing within the constraints dictated by the National Curriculum (as explained in Chapter Three). Schools will always need, for example, books on Greeks or Romans but they don't want just more of the same.

Remember, though, that the Curriculum is developing and changing all the time. While this provides one of the greatest challenges for teachers, it should provide the greatest opportunity for new writers. By anticipating curriculum changes in advance of implementation, writers can come up with brand-new material and be first in line to offer it to publishers, who, hopefully, will already have assessed the potential market.

However, as well as traditional non-fiction publishing, high-street publishers are looking for fresh subject matter for their non-fiction lists and this has resulted in some successful one-offs. *Can You Feel the Force?* (Richard Hammond) has been snapped up by libraries and schools as much as by high-street retailers. It taps into fun experimentation now going on in the playground – such as creating huge amounts of foam simply by putting a certain sweet into a fizzy drink.

Interactivity is now key in non-fiction across all ages. Non-fiction with added extras, such as lift-the-flap features, appeal to the gift market, but can also fill a slot in books for homework.

The picture concept is also vital. The difference between a good non-fiction title and a bad one often comes down to the quality of the artwork. Scholastic, for example, has virtually reinvented its *Horrible Histories* series by taking the original black-and-white illustrations into colour.

As a new writer, however, it is important not to go overboard on the 'gimmick' factor. The best way forward is to try to come up with a strong and different book that has practical, factual information and an educational purpose as well as entertainment value.

If writing pure information books isn't really your thing, you could try your hand at a growing trend in this market – that of narrative non-fiction, or 'faction'. This trend started with the *Ology* books from Templar, which use a non-fiction format but with a narrative running through them. Other publishers are jumping on the bandwagon and new 'faction' titles can be as simple as a story presented alongside factual information (e.g. Walker Books *Read and Wonder* series) or resemble the more complicated *Lifelines* (published by Kingfisher). Each title in the *Lifeline* series is based on fictional characters from a real time in history but also includes a section on historical events and a more traditional reference section about life in that particular period. 'Faction' can be adapted for all ages and is certainly set to shake up the non-fiction market going forward.

Lastly, on this subject of what to write about, it is worth keeping one eye on what is working in the adult non-ficition market. Lynne Truss has brought out a children's version of her adult bestseller *Eats, Shoots & Leaves,* Michael van Straten has pulled off a similar feat with his *Super Juice for Kids* and, following hot on the heels of all those celebrity cookbooks for adults, *Star Cooks* (Dorling Kindersley) offers children their own collection of celebrity recipes. If you can pick up on information trends that are working for adults then it may be perfectly possible to turn these ideas around and make them work for kids.

Is it Accurate?

A common misconception among new writers is that the children's non-fiction market is only open to 'experts'. This is quite definitely not the case. Chris Knowles, for example, worked for London Transport prior to making his big break with *The Paper Shoe Book*. In fact, not being an expert when you start can even be an asset. Chances are you will not regard some areas of your chosen topic as 'too obvious' to include when these are precisely the areas that are not in the least bit obvious to a child.

However, although you do not need to be an expert, it should go without saying that any work of non-fiction needs to be accurate. If you are not professionally qualified in the field about which you have chosen to write then make sure that someone who *is* qualified vets your work for accuracy *before* you submit it. On the other hand, if you do have professional qualifications in your chosen field then make sure the publishers know it. Include relevant information about yourself in your covering letter in order to reassure the editor about the accuracy of your work.

Remember, though, that while you can allocate yourself an area of expertise and market yourself as a writer with a sound knowledge of a particular subject, never lose sight of the fact that you are not selling yourself, but your idea. The publisher's priority, after all, is to sell a creative concept to the general public – who you are is irrelevant.

And on the subject of submitting ideas to a publisher, don't be precious with them. Publishers are professionals – they won't plagiarise your creativity. It is better to submit a list of a dozen or more ideas to prove that you are versatile and blessed with a fertile imagination. Remember, though, that if you are submitting several proposals, you need to keep them as concise as possible.

Is it Stylish?

Many writers have a problem with the actual writing skills involved in children's non-fiction. It is every bit as important for a non-fiction book to be written in a lively and interesting style, and to have an eye-catching title and opening sentence, as a fiction book. Even children motivated by an interest in the subject matter will turn away if the book is inappropriate for their age or reading level, or simply a dull recounting of facts. Use active verbs and keep it lively. Don't be afraid of using appropriate humour if you need to.

As when writing a Picture Book, your writing should have an appealing sound and rhythm. Read your work aloud, recording it if necessary, to get a feel for how your sentences sound. Every word has to earn its place on the page, especially when writing for very young children.

Small chunks of text with headings, or information presented in boxes or sidebars, may work better than pages of text. The same amount of information may be there, but in smaller chunks it is easier to read and absorb. It also enables children to practise the all-important art of skimming for information.

Experiment with different forms in which to present information. This could include a question-and-answer format, quizzes, puzzles, games and activities, as well as narratives.

Is it Organised?

Lack of clarity is another problem many writers come up against when putting together a non-fiction idea. Organising your work to make it easier for children to access is good practice. Use chapters, and headings and subheadings within chapters, and include a contents page and an index to make your book easier to navigate. A glossary to explain any technical terms will make it easier to understand and also make it more saleable to the schools market since the use of these parts of a book is part of the Literacy Hour requirements in primary schools.

When organising your work, you have a wide range of choices. These include, though they are not limited to:

- Chronological: moving from past, through the present, and towards the future – particularly appropriate for work based in history, or for work that aims to recount something.
- Spatial: connecting your topics by their relation to each other in space – useful for work about, for example, ecosystems such as a forest or the ocean.
- Cause and effect: useful for science-based work, or for work that seeks to persuade or discuss.
- Step-by-step: useful for work to do with instructions.
- Reasoning: moving from specific examples to a general conclusion (induction) or from generalisation to conclusion using specific cases (deduction) – useful for persuasive or discussion work.
- Problem and solution: useful for reference, reports, instructions.

Packagers

Packagers operate in a different way to publishers and are often more receptive to novelty books because the way they sell their product means that they can afford the high expenses involved in producing such books.

Books like *The Paper Shoe Book* go way beyond the cost parameters set by traditional publishers for their own markets. The packager, on the other hand, matches the expertise of specialist writers, artists and photographers with the professional craftsmanship of in-house editors and art editors, and then recoups the cost of the 'package' by pre-selling rights in the titles to publishers throughout the world: what is known as a 'co-edition'. Co-editions are often complicated to produce and manage, because of the time and co-ordination involved, so specialist knowledge of how they work is vital.

There are a number of packagers dealing in children's books and a comprehensive up-to-date list can be found in *The Children's Writers' & Artists' Yearbook.*

MAGAZINES

There are a number of children's and teenage magazines on the market that depend upon freelance contributions.

If you think you would like to write for this market, the first thing you need to do is to check out which magazines are currently out there. This sector of the publishing industry is incredibly fickle and if I mention any titles at the time of writing this, like as not they will be gone by the time this book is actually published. Use guides such as *The Children's Writers' & Artists' Yearbook,* making sure, of course, that you always refer to the most up-to-date edition.

Having given the market a brief 'overview', you now need to study it in more depth. Select any magazines that interest you and make a quick phone call to find out if they accept freelance contributions. Some magazines will originate ideas in-house and only commission pieces from writers already known to them; or it will have a team of staff writers who provide all the non-fiction copy.

While you're making that phone call, and if they do indeed welcome unsolicited, freelance submissions, it could be worthwhile asking if the magazine has a particular day on which they brainstorm ideas. If you can time your proposal to land on the editor's desk just as he/she is wracking his/her brain for new ideas for the next edition then you are in with a much better chance of being noticed. A long shot, I know, but worth a try.

Alternatively, if you have a specialist area – perhaps you work at Battersea Dogs' Home and have always fancied penning an article for *Your Dog* magazine – then try persuading the editor to meet up with you to discuss your ideas. Even if nothing comes of the meeting initially, you will, hopefully, have impressed the editor sufficiently so that your name is top of the list when it comes to commissioning articles in the future.

Whatever your approach, when you do finally decide to target a particular magazine make sure you read it inside and out before you go any further. Read it, familiarise yourself with the content, soak up the tone of the language used. You're never going to place that piece on 'Crocheting for Beginners' if the magazine only features tragic real-life stories or articles on seduction techniques.

When searching around for ideas, think about the timing of the magazine's publication. If it is weekly, you need to show that you have your finger on the pulse, so consider what is currently 'hot'. For example, what's showing on TV, what's on at the cinema, who's in the gossip pages, what's happening at school? If your chosen magazine is monthly then look at a selection of back issues and think about how you could give a new spin to a well-worn theme. And, whatever the frequency of the publication, never underestimate the influence of the seasons. They do, after all, affect how we live our lives so they should affect what you write about as well.

As with non-fiction books, you do not need to write the whole thing before approaching a magazine editor. A professionally written covering letter, accompanied by a catchy headline and a brief synopsis, speaks volumes and will be looked on far more favourably than a folder bursting with completed articles.

Non-Fiction: Exercises
- Look at the adult non-fiction market and choose a title that could be adapted to suit children.
- Think about how you are going to organise your material (see section above, *Is it Organised?*). Write a one- or two-paragraph synopsis and then rough out a detailed plan.
- Select a children's or teen magazine and come up with an idea for a piece or article. Write a catchy title and brief synopsis of your idea.

CHAPTER EIGHT

POETRY

My poem's enclosed
for you to see.
If they're worth printing
talk to me.
Give me a ring
to fix a date.
We'll set a time
Please don't be late.
If you aren't impressed, however
return to sender.
I'll put them out
again to tender!

This witty ditty landed on my desk, along with several poems. It certainly made me laugh and the accompanying poems were of good quality. But as an editor I needed to know more – a *lot* more – before I could even start to consider these poems seriously. Remember that poetry is a difficult market to break into because it is, by its very nature, a niche market.

AGE RANGE

The poetry editor, once he/she has decided that a collection of poems has potential, will first of all consider the age range for which the author is writing. Those of you who think poetry should be ageless are right: good poetry can be enjoyed right across the board. Elderly people still enjoy nursery rhymes; very young children will often display a surprisingly sophisticated taste in poetry. However, it is important that the poet has some sort of target audience in mind.

Generally speaking, children's poetry can be divided into three distinct categories: poetry for the 6–10 age range, poetry for the 10–12 age range, and teenage/young adult poetry. Poetry for the under-sixes tends to be published in the form of Picture Books rather than straightforward poetry. (It is also worth mentioning, at this point, that teenage poetry is a small market – and extremely hard to enter.)

EXPERIENCE

Having assessed the age range for which the poet is writing, the next big stumbling block is experience. By this I don't, necessarily, mean publishing experience – but it obviously helps if your poetry has had some kind of a public airing, in magazines, newspapers or through small presses.

As I mentioned in Chapter One, one of the ways in which publishers make children's books economically viable is by organising co-editions so that the book can be sold in different countries, sometimes being translated into different languages. However, it is almost impossible to interest foreign publishers in British poetry collections. This is partly down to translation problems but, also, poetry has proven to be a very individual medium as far as different cultures are concerned. So in order for a British publisher to recoup their costs on a poetry collection, the publisher must rely on sizeable sales in the UK alone. And in order to achieve good sales, the poet him/herself needs to have earned a reputation and be a household name *before* their poetry is published.

Many of today's top children's poets wrote for adults before they moved into the children's arena. In order to be taken seriously, it is important to show publishers that you are a 'Poet' with a capital 'P' and that you are committed to your chosen artform. Otherwise, not only will you find that there are limited openings but, also, that you do not have the correct credentials deemed necessary to make it in the world of poetry. For example, John Aigard and Jackie Kay were both published by Blood Axe (a long-established and well-respected adult poetry small press) prior to being published by Puffin Books.

The Poetry Society (22 Betterton Street, London WC2H 9BU) is an excellent resource for the new poet. They, too, stress the importance of gaining experience before approaching publishers, saying – and I quote – 'no publisher is going to go near an unknown name'.

They suggest building up a portfolio, including magazines or other publications in which your poetry has appeared and lists of readings and festivals with which you have been involved. They provide advice on how to gain access to all those opportunities.

It is particularly interesting to note that the Poetry Society's information sheet on children's poetry publishers only lists thirteen major names. If you consider that there are over one hundred children's book publishers, it gives some idea as to the difficulty of breaking in to this particular genre.

Performance

These days the children's poet must not only enjoy performing their own poetry, but they must be good at it. They must also be prepared to commit large amounts of their time to touring schools, bookshops, libraries and festivals in order to read and promote their work. Live performance is considered to be a vital part of any poet's CV and the importance of performance is more or less written into most poets' contracts. To underline this point, take this small clip lifted from the Puffin catalogue describing poet Gervase Phinn: 'Collection of children's poetry from a former teacher and school inspector, who is renowned all over the UK for his live performances . . .'

So try to get out and about *reading* your poetry to as many groups as possible. In particular, try to get into schools. Schools, these days, are quite rightly very security conscious, so you will need to go through the right channels with a letter to the Literacy Co-Ordinator, copied to the Head Teacher, explaining what you have to offer and what you would like to achieve from your visit. However, school visits give visiting poets an opportunity not only to try out their poems, but also the opportunity to speak to the children and familiarise themselves with language trends and interests.

It is important, to stand any chance of being taken seriously by a publisher, that you build up some sort of 'fan base' – however small. Along with your portfolio you can then mention this performance experience when approaching publishers with your work. Lindsay MacRae says that she started out as a performance poet of adult poetry and describes herself, back then, as 'the angry young woman' performing politically slanted poetry in alternative cabaret clubs and pubs.

But being, first and foremost, a performer, helps MacRae to write her poetry. Reading poetry out loud helps a writer get a sense of rhythm; to discover which words resonate with power and emotion, and which poems are likely to earn a positive response from an audience/readership. Children respond particularly well to poems with strong rhythms, humour and plenty of dialogue featuring characters speaking in different voices. Lindsay MacRae's poems often start out as imagined conversations and develop from there:

> 'I *insist* on paying,' said Doris
> 'It's *my* treat!' shrieks Mum,
> shoving the sweaty £20 note back at her.
> '*Please* let me pay,' begs Doris,
> scrunching up the note and shoving it
> in Mum's pocket.
>
> From *High Noon at Barking Odeon*

One can easily imagine how hilarious this 'strange adult conflict' would become when performed.

MacRae does stress, however, that a contrast of styles is important and that one wildly hilarious poem after another would become wearing, even in performance. Her collections range from the scatological *Dog Poo Haiku* to the much more sombre and serious *Children Also Get Depressed*.

She is convinced that the fact she is young and a woman has contributed to her success in the children's poetry field. Many of today's children's writers are older men and, while their poetry continues to be brilliantly inspiring, there is a distinct lack of female poets and poets from multi-cultural backgrounds.

MacRae's advice to the aspiring children's poet is to get out there and to build up a following. You'll soon find out if you've got what it takes to perform – and if your poems work in front of a young, live audience with very frank theories on what is boring and what isn't, they will work anywhere.

USING THE INTERNET

Another way to maintain and build up a fan base is to build a personalised website – something that many publishers ask of their authors anyway, whatever market they are writing for. You can do this very simply by creating a page on something like myspace.com or go the whole hog and build a website of your own from scratch. Whichever way you go, remember that sites for this age group need to be fresh, funky and interactive as well as intuitively navigable.

Once you have your website up and running, you can use it to publish your poetry, sell your collections, publicise your availability as a performer and so on. Many publishers agree that feeling as if you are part of an online community is part of the fun of the Internet: blogging and forum-style websites are great ways of spreading the word about your poems.

VOICE

When writing poetry for children, as in any other form of children's writing, it's essential to keep the requirements of the audience in mind. A children's poem can be about anything, but should be presented through a 'child's eye view'. Children like poems about their own lives (think, for example, of the sharp observation of school life in *Please Mrs Butler* and *Heard it in the Playground*, both by Allan Ahlberg) or about their interests, e.g. space travel, animals, ghosts.

There should be vivid visual detail, plus humour is an important ingredient, even in the presentation of serious subjects. Although I don't want you to worry too much at this stage about the technical side of writing poetry, remember that a poem should have shape even when you're writing 'free verse', i.e. without a fixed rhythm and rhyme scheme.

You should also be aware of what other poets, for both adults and children, are doing. After all, if you don't read poetry, why would you want to write it? Fashions change, and what was publishable fifty years ago might not be so today.

Readers of unsolicited poetry will be looking for a distinctive voice, which makes you, as a poet, unique. Remember that your voice has to appeal to the child of today. This question of 'voice' or 'style' is always a thorny one; even published poets agree that it is hard not to be influenced by the style of others.

I would suggest examining what makes you stand out from the crowd and emphasise those individual qualities. Jackie Kay, for example, uses idiomatic language and the Scottish dialect to great effect:

> But see when Sleekit is discovered for her cunning wit . . .
> What does she do first? Blame it on Greta, Jimmy, Jo, Gillian, or worse,
> Her tiny toty week sister (shame)
> Who screams in a big voice for her wee wean:
> WISNAE ME WISNAE ME WIS HER AGAIN
> WISNAE ME WISNAE ME WIS HER AGAIN
>
> From *Sleekit*

ANTHOLOGIES

As a new poetry writer, your best chance of publishing success lies with poetry anthologies. These are usually themed and sales rely on the reputation of the publisher and the anthologist – which makes including new 'names' a lot less risky. Poetry anthologists hold their own lists of poets whom they like to use, plus they will approach agents looking for suitable contributions.

If you don't have an agent, the best way to approach anthologists is by writing to them care of the relevant publishing house. So, for example, if during your research you see that John Foster has done a number of collections for Oxford University Press, you would write to John care of Oxford University Press.

Publishers are always happy to forward communications to their authors.

Write to anthologists using the approach guidelines above. Enclose, say, five poems illustrating your work and ask to be kept in mind for future anthologies that they may be preparing. Anthologists are usually delighted to discover new, fresh voices and, if a poet is good enough, they will be used.

Once you have a poem accepted into an anthology, it will be very often picked up and used in other, forthcoming anthologies.

SUBMISSION

So you've won a couple of competitions, your poems have been published in a few specialist magazines, and hordes of children are besieging you, *begging* to know where they can buy your first collection. *Now* is the time to approach a publisher.

No poetry editor wants to be deluged with the entire contents of your life's work. Personally, I like to see no more than twelve poems, 'grouped' or 'themed' in some way, which can help to give your collection focus. For example, all the poems in one of Brian Patten's collections, *Utter Nutters*, are based around one particular street. It's not essential, however, to find a theme if your poems only seem to work as separate entities.

It is important that children's poets make the distinction between 'verse' and 'poetry'; children's poetry publishers are in the business of publishing saleable collections of poetry, not greetings cards! Nor are most poetry editors looking for picture-book material.

At the end of the day, what really matters is the reaction to poetry of the children themselves. Because children's poetry today is so relevant and accessible it will often provide reluctant readers with their first insight that books can be fun.

Consider the words of children's poetry anthologist, Anne Harvey: 'Look for the best from the past and present. Offer children what will stretch imagination and add to experience, widen horizons, deepen their feelings, enliven their senses.'

Or, to put it another way:

I would speak great poems
With me great big voice
Great big hugs and kisses
Would make me feel nice
This great world would work together
     as a team
I would live for ever
In me great big dream
From *Once Upon a Time* by Benjamin Zephaniah

Poetry: Exercises

- Pay a visit to your local children's library or bookshop and have a browse through all the most recently published poetry books – collections by single poets and themed anthologies.
- Choose an anthology that you like and imagine that you have been approached to contribute one more poem to the collection. Write a poem that seems to you to fit with the mood of the collection.
- Think about your style of writing, or 'voice', and choose a subject around which you could centre your own collection of poems.

CHAPTER NINE

SELF-PUBLISHING

In the first edition of this book, I wouldn't have dreamed of including a chapter on self-publishing. Back then the only children's writers who self-published were those with more money than sense, and egos to match. However, times have changed over the last ten years and we have entered a new age of publishing technology, which means that self-publishing is a very real option for everyone and can sometimes even be the most appropriate route to take.

WHAT IS SELF-PUBLISHING?

Self-publishing is, quite literally, just that – you publish your own work. In other words, you, the author, are taking direct responsibility for the writing, production, marketing and sales of your book. It's true that you may decide to enlist the help of experts in any one, or more, of these fields (indeed I would suggest that you do) but, ultimately, you are taking personal responsibility for the completed publication of your book. You are also funding publication out of your own pocket.

The alternative to self-publishing is what I would term 'retail publishing' or 'mainstream publishing'. Authors whose books are accepted by a mainstream publisher will enter into an agreement with that publisher whereby the publisher will undertake full responsibility for every aspect of publication. They will do this at their own cost and will remunerate you, the author, on a royalty basis.

Put simply, in self-publishing you pay money to get your work published, whereas in mainstream publishing money gets paid to you. Of course, it may be that your self-published book goes on to make a huge profit and you recoup any money that you paid out and more. However, in self-publishing it is you, the author, who is taking the financial risk, in the first instance, rather than a third party.

Reasons to Self-publish

Okay, so you've written your children's book and you're convinced that it's going to be the next *Harry Potter*. Sadly, however, no one else seems to agree with you. You've not only approached every publisher in *The Writers' & Artists' Yearbook* but every agent as well and it's been rejection and knock-backs all the way down the line.

At this point, you have three choices – you can give up entirely, you can pick yourself up and try again or you can self-publish.

Very often a children's author may have written something specifically for their children or grandchildren. It may not be marketable enough to be taken on by one of the big guns but the author wants to go ahead anyway as they know that they will be able to sell it to family and friends. This is fine as long as you accept that you are very unlikely to recoup your costs, let alone make a profit. However, for these types of writers, personal satisfaction far outweighs any monetary considerations.

Other writers may be tackling subjects that, although of enormous interest to a small percentage of the population, hold absolutely no interest at all to anyone else. This very often happens when someone has experience of a child suffering from a little-known illness or disability. With all the best will in the world, a mainstream publisher won't be prepared to take on this type of project as they know, realistically, that sales will be too small to make it worthwhile (and publishers are businesses, not charities – something that too many new writers forget!).

In cases such as these it may be possible for the author to generate sufficient sales themselves through, say, supporting charities and groups connected to their specialist subject. Indeed, charities are sometimes interested in helping to finance such projects themselves.

Children's poets have good reasons to self-publish collections of their own poetry. As discussed in the previous chapter, children's poets need to build up a fan base *before* they can be considered seriously by a publisher. Printing copies of their poetry to give away at readings is an excellent way of marketing and selling their own work.

It should be noted that there are, also, good reasons *not* to self-publish. The biggest one is the erroneous belief that a mainstream publisher is more likely to pick up on a self-published book than on a 'virgin' manuscript. This is not true. Indeed, I would go as far as to say that the opposite is true.

Publishers and agents are generally suspicious of self-published submissions. Fairly, or unfairly, they will suspect that the writer has already tried publishers with his original manuscript and, having failed, has turned to self-publishing. Even if the work is good, the publisher may feel that, having dipped their toes in the murky waters that are 'sales', the writer has 'spoiled' any potential market for the publisher.

It is true to say, however, that in the States mainstream publishers regularly trawl through self-published lists, and as many as one in ten new children's authors are 'discovered' in this way. So although, in this country, publishers and agents are currently dismissive of self-published work it could well be that the situation will change – especially with fewer and fewer publishers being prepared to place their money on anything other than betting certainties.

The single, best reason to self-publish your book is because you believe in your own work and you also know that you have the ability to market it successfully. The most difficult books to self-publish are those that appeal to everyone. However, if you can define your market, and work out how to access that market, you will be a long way along the route to self-publishing success.

Self-publishing Options

The simplest way to self-publish is by using a printer, a photocopier and a staple gun. In this way you can type up your manuscript and put together a few booklets to distribute to anyone who is interested. As I said, it's simple, it's cheap and it works.

If that's not your idea of publishing a 'proper book' then the next simplest way to self-publish is by buying your own publishing equipment and 'printing on demand'. 'Print on demand' (POD) is relatively new and it's gaining momentum all the time. The idea is that books can be published as and when they are needed – one at a time if necessary. So instead of estimating the size of your print run in advance, you can lie back and let the market decide. Less risk, but using this type of technology is an expensive investment and isn't everyone's cup of tea.

Another new and simple way of getting published is to place your writing on the Internet. You can either put it on your own website, or find someone who will add it to theirs. This is known as an 'ebook' and it can then be downloaded onto palmheld computers, laptops and iPods etc. This method could work well if you are very computer literate and writing for the older child where you can establish some kind of cult following.

However, for writers who believe that nothing can ever replace the printed book and want to see their writing in a 'proper' published format, a reputable self-publishing company may be the answer. By this I do *not* mean a vanity publisher.

'Vanity publishing' is the name given to services offered by rather less scrupulous publishing companies. These publishers misrepresent their services for the sole purpose of making large sums of money dishonestly. You can usually spot them as they will almost always return your manuscript with an extremely flattering (and extremely short) 'reader's report', which will praise your work to the skies, claim that it will sell in its millions with their help and then demand extortionate sums of money to publish it (sometimes as much as £10,000).

Reputable self-publishing companies, on the other hand, offer an honest, upfront service to publish your book in return for money. They will never make false claims about the likelihood of your recouping your costs (indeed, the best ones warn that you *won't* recoup your costs – particularly with a children's book) and will usually show a clear break down of their services and the fees that they charge for each stage of the publishing process. In this way, you can sometimes achieve a more reasonable rate if you decided to take on, say, distribution and promotion yourself, or forego their copy-editing services.

The last option open to you, if you still want to self-publish, is to go it alone. The publishing process is complicated and fraught with difficulties and, in this chapter, I have only the space to provide a brief overview. However, if this is a route that you want to take there are books and publications out there that can help and these are listed in Chapter Seventeen towards the end of this book.

Going It Alone

The first thing to do is to define your readership and your market. Decide which age group you are writing for and what format your book is going to take. Is it going to be illustrated and, if so, are you going to illustrate the book yourself, commission someone else to do the illustrations or use 'clip art'.

Next you need to write your book (obviously!), edit it, rewrite it and then, most probably, repeat steps two and three many times over. I can't stress enough how important it is to get things right at this stage as any major changes later on will cost money and could put the whole project at risk.

If you have a computer (and if you haven't got one I would suggest that you go out and buy one) you can word-process your own manuscript, showing where any illustrations are going to go. It can then be delivered to the printer 'on disc' and they can typeset it for you.

When self-publishing a children's book, how the book 'looks' is going to be very important. Book design and book production are specialist areas so, at this point, it is probably wise to enlist the help of a specialist self-publishing service provider. They will charge but I would suggest that it will be money well spent. Alternatively, if you feel up to it, you could buy your own design software – typical examples are PageMaker, QuarkXPress and InDesign.

If you are not sure how you want your book to look, select an already published book that meets your perceived requirements. You can then ask the designer to follow a similar format.

This is particularly helpful when planning an illustrated book for the younger end of the market.

Finding a printer is your next hurdle. As with book design and production, you could use an established self-publishing company, or you could find your own printer.

If you go the latter route, you are looking for a small print shop that is used to producing finished work to the standard you need. Questions you need to ask your printer are: Can they take camera-ready artwork? Can they produce the finished article or will you have to find a binder? And, Can they do small print runs?

The standard way of quoting for a print run is to give a price for the number of copies produced, and a price for a 'run on'. These are extra copies after they have set up the first batch, and the price you will pay if the book is a runaway success and you need more copies printed.

Be prudent when it comes to deciding upon your initial print run. Remember that printing more than will be sold will cost you more in the long run. The cost of short-run reprints is sufficiently cheap to encourage conservative printing in the first place.

Jacket design is another important consideration – particularly when producing a children's book. If you talk to children, you will find that they have strong views on what makes for good cover design. Among things that children don't like are faces staring straight out of the cover (the argument being that if they don't like the look of the face they won't like the story), bright pink covers and covers that have nothing to do with the story content. Design features that they do like are simple photographs and strong, simple graphics – the starker the better.

The book blurb is another vital ingredient. This is normally printed on the back cover and/or the first page. Remember that if a child gets as far as reading the blurb they are seriously considering reading the book and how persuasive your blurb is, is going to tip them one way or the other.

Don't waste words. Starting with 'This book' is not on – no one is going to dispute that it is a book or even this particular one. Blurbs should be short (no more than 200 words maximum), to the point, say what the book is about but not give too much away. Easy!

Nitty Gritty Stuff

As well as getting your book up and running, there are also various boring, but necessary, legal niceties to consider – what I call the nitty gritty side to self-publishing.

Many self-published books are produced to look as though they might have been produced commercially and this can easily be done by coming up with your own imprint name and including it on the jacket. The fact that your publishing empire is just you and your cat doesn't mean that you can't present a professional front to the world.

Businesses in the UK can be of several types although you will probably choose to work as a Sole Trader. This means that you adopt a business name and become an official 'Small Press'. Any profits can be declared on your personal tax return and you can offset some operating expenses against tax.

Your business should have an address and you should include these details on the back of your book and, preferably, inside as well. This makes it easier for people to contact you and, hopefully, place orders. If you are uneasy about using your home address you can use a PO box number or an official mailing address.

As well as these details, each book you produce will also need an ISBN and Barcode. An ISBN (International Standard Book Number) is not essential but if you intend to sell your book professionally it is advisable. The British Library, libraries, book wholesalers and bookshops use the ISBN as a unique reference number to record information about the book on their computer systems and Barcodes are based on the ISBN. You can contact the ISBN agency at www.isbn.nielsenbookdata.co.uk.

Nielsen BookData helps publishers sell books by making sure booksellers have the most accurate, comprehensive and up-to-date information available about your title. It requires the type of information that helps identify, find, order and sell your books. The ISBN, author, title, date of publication and price are essential, but there can be much more.

For instance, a description of the content, a short biography of the author, the cover image, the format of the book and a standard subject code to help booksellers searching in a specific subject area can be provided. You can tell them who distributes your book, the markets in which they are available and much more. Nielsen BookData can be contacted at www.bookdata.co.uk.

Lastly, you need to price your book – although, in reality, this should have already been decided when you printed your book cover. A book is traditionally priced at five times its production cost. Small presses (you would fall into this category) normally have to settle for three times the production cost as their costs are proportionally higher.

If you choose to sell through bookshops, they will demand a minimum of 35% of the cover price and they get this in the form of a discount. As the publisher, you get the rest (assuming you have written the book yourself) after you have paid all your costs. So do some sums and calculate a price that will avoid you becoming bankrupt. Remember, though, that your readers won't want to break the bank to buy your book, so price it sensibly.

Selling Your Book

This is when you find out why the big publishers only bet on certainties. You will have to use every marketing trick you can dream up to get your title noticed. Remember, bookshop managers are used to dealing with sales reps from the big publishers who have advertising money to burn, so they're not going to be impressed by someone with a couple of paperbacks in a carrier bag.

The moment you know you are going to self-publish, start building a mailing list of friends and contacts who might be persuaded to buy your book. This should also include the names of anyone to whom you could send a review copy when the time comes.

Prepare an eye-catching flier and get it out to all your contacts ahead of publication. Include a mail-order option on the flier to maximise sales.

On publication day organise a launch party and invite all your friends and contacts. Make sure you have plenty of copies of your book to sell at the party and offer to personalize copies by signing them.

Offer to do free readings in schools and libraries. This will not only whip up interest in you, as an author, but will also create a good point of sale for your book.

Most schools nowadays organise fundraising fêtes and fairs at least once a term. In return for a percentage of the sales, these schools may well be happy for you to set up a stall selling your book.

If you are going to approach booksellers, target local book-shops first. Many smaller bookshops are happy to feature the work of local authors as part of their window display.

Lastly, in order to promote your book, you could consider taking a stall at one of the book fairs that take place around the world – London being the most obvious choice for those living in the UK. It's likely to be an expensive option but could pay dividends.

Self-published children's author Frank Hinks took a stall at the London Book Fair in 2003. His first visitor was Korean literary agent, Jeffrey Kim, and as a result of that visit the Korean translation rights of Frank's first series of children's books was bought by Marubol Publishing.

Following their first meeting, Jeffrey Kim sent Frank a list of the various authors the agency represented. The list included Che Guevara, the Dalai Lama, Umberto Eco and Virginia Woolf.

Says Frank, 'I have yet to make my fortune in self-publishing but in such distinguished company who knows what the future may bring!'

OTHER SUCCESS STORIES

However much you may wish to see your work in print, I hope you will have realised by now that self-publishing is a long way from being the ideal answer. I haven't really talked about the costs of publishing your own work because exact cost depends on so many different factors – how long, how many illustrations, full colour or black and white, print runs etc. Rest assured though, that whatever type of book you wish to publish, you are talking an absolute *minimum* of £1500.

But for some authors, self-publishing has opened doors to a world that they could previously only dream of. A few years ago

G. P. Taylor – a 43-year-old Yorkshire vicar – sold his beloved motorbike to pay for his children's novel *Shadowmancer* to be self-published. The book has been a runaway success. There's a movie deal, television shows and a book contract big enough to warrant non-disclosure clauses. In the past few years he has made millions.

Another 43-year-old – John Howard from East Sussex – became so disillusioned by the fact that most publishers didn't even read his manuscript that he published *The Key to Chintak* himself. This book is aimed at the 10-plus market and tells the story of a 12-year-old girl who can read the pages of a blank book that no one else can see. She sets off with her grandfather on an adventure to find the trapped children who wrote the book.

After visiting forty schools with his book, he found himself inundated with thousands of orders before discovering that it had also caught the eye of buyers at Waterstone's and WHSmith, both of which decided to stock it.

Three film companies, including the Hollywood heavyweight Miramax, have shown interest, seven international publishers have approached him about the foreign rights and British companies are asking about the second and third editions.

Children's author, Louise Dale, has so successfully self-published her *Time Trigger* series, under her own Dragonheart Publishing imprint, that she is now just starting to publish other authors. In other words, it is sometimes possible to make the progression from self-publisher to small press to something akin to mainstream publishing.

EXERCISES

- Come up with an idea that you think may lend itself to self-publishing.
- Decide upon the format that your book is going to take.
- Write a book 'blurb' of no more than 200 words that you could put on the back cover of your published book.
- Identify your potential market and come up with three different marketing strategies. Try to think 'outside the box' and be as creative as possible.

II

GET WRITING!

CHAPTER TEN

SUBJECT MATTER

Once an author has studied the market they hope to write for, they must decide what they want to write *about*.

If you have studied the first part of this book carefully, and completed some of the exercises at the end of each chapter, you will, by now, have a good idea of the different types of children's book currently being sold. You may even already have decided what type of book you want to write, or identified a gap in the market that you want to fill.

Alternatively, you may be feeling punch-drunk on the sheer enormity of the market; perhaps you are thinking that every subject under the sun has already been covered and that not even the mighty J. K. Rowling could come up with anything new or different.

If you fall into this last category, relax. Fact is, in all probability, every subject under the sun *has* already been covered. This doesn't mean, however, that there is nothing left for you to write about. Margret Geraghty, in her excellent *Novelist's Guide*, compared fiction to the fashion business: 'Just as Westwood [fashion designer] might take a plain dress and cover it with chicken wire, so can writers take a basic plot and develop it afresh.'

WHAT CAN I WRITE ABOUT?

The first thing to do is to come up with an idea you feel really enthusiastic about and *then* worry about whether it has been done before and, if so, how it was tackled. Some writers argue that there are only a limited number of plots that human ingenuity can feasibly contrive: originality consists of 'customising' them and coming up with a new angle to satisfy the needs of the current market.

There is no doubt that, in children's publishing as in adult publishing, there are 'trends' for certain types of books. Books about forest animals may be popular one year, only to be replaced by school stories the next. There is really no easy way to get to grips with what is popular and what isn't – all I can do here is point out the possible pitfalls of various topic areas, so that you are aware of the lie of the land before you start.

Historical Fiction

Because of the amount of research involved, Historical Fiction is probably the most arduous market of all for the children's writer. There is little point spending months working on an idea if ultimately it has mimimal chance of acceptance. Having said that, this area is slowly coming back into favour with publishers.

Time-Slip Stories

These are an 'accessible' way of dealing with historical issues. Time-Slip Stories tend to start in the present and move backwards in time, or vice-versa. Very often they tell stories of two different sets of characters, living in parallel universes in time, yet connected in some way. These types of stories are less popular than they used to be mainly because it is *extremely* hard to make them plausible. Although not a children's book, for me one of the best Time-Slip Stories out there is *The Time Traveler's Wife* by Audrey Niffenegger. Call me gullible but I *totally* believed in it. I'd love to see something similar done for children.

Fantasy

A popular area with a strong following. But *Lord of the Rings* fans beware! There are a number of highly successful writers of 'straight' Fantasy around but it is difficult to excel in this area simply because a new Fantasy novel has to compete against extremely stiff competition. Plus the market is rather overloaded, at the moment, with hefty trilogies.

Fantasy also seems to attract extreme reactions: readers either love it or loathe it, so the market is very polarised. However, it is possible to focus on the 'non-fantasy' elements of your story to give those who 'loathe' Fantasy something to hook into, while fulfilling the more specific requirements of established Fantasy fans. Harry Potter is a good example of this.

Science Fiction
This is another 'love it or loathe it' area, I'm afraid. As with Fantasy, it is best to write a Science Fiction Story that even non-believers can enjoy. The secret is to keep the storyline as non-technical as possible – too much detail about the inner workings of spaceships can be off-putting for the sceptics.

Fairy Tales
The mistake some new authors make with Fairy Tales is to update old Fairy Tales by giving them a modern-day slant. This has been done so often it is now hard to give any traditional story an original angle. If I could have a pound for every time I've read about a princess who likes climbing tress, or a prince who rides a motorbike rather than a horse, I'd be a rich woman!

Adventure Stories
These are plot-driven, action-based books but, too often, new writers try to imitate Enid Blyton. I'm afraid it's a question of 'been there, done that, time to move on'. Make no mistake, Blyton wrote wonderful, pacey, stream-lined stories, but today's publishers demand more than this type of one-dimensional plot. It is much better if an adventure story has some real relevance to modern life. For example, Malorie Blackman's *Hacker*, as the title suggests, features computers and a girl's fight to free her father from prison – a sort of updated *Railway Children*. Catherine MacPhail's *Run Zan Run* features a girl's fight against serious bullying helped by a homeless runaway. In both these books, it is the adventure that drives the plot, but that doesn't stop either author from examining other issues as well.

War Books

Another area that has, in my opinion, been rather overdone – particularly when writing about the First and Second World Wars. That's not to say that there aren't some stunning books around about the two World Wars, but it does mean that in order to get your war book accepted it has to be even *more* stunning, which will be hard when you take into account books such as *Private Peaceful* by Michael Morpurgo (HarperCollins). If you are absolutely intent on writing a War Book, I would suggest looking at more recent skirmishes for inspiration. After all, War books don't get much better than Meg Rosoff's *How I Live Now* (Puffin), which is about an entirely fictional war set in the future.

Horror and Ghost Books

Plausibility is the biggest problem with Horror and Ghost Books. It is all too easy to slip into melodrama, which will, at best, seem funny or, at worst, ridiculous. As with adventure books, the best Horror and Ghost Stories set out to do more than just horrify or frighten – they will often explore other issues, and, in particular, the success of their plots will depend upon strong characterisation. Unless you really enjoy reading this type of book yourself, I wouldn't even attempt to try.

Funny Books

Being deliberately 'funny' in writing is probably the hardest thing of all to achieve. What makes someone laugh is very personal and subjective, writers either tend to go right over the top, or are so subtle the humour gets missed. If you would like to write a funny book, I suggest you look carefully at books that make you laugh and try to work out just *why* it is so humorous. Sometimes this will mean dissecting a particular sentence bit by bit; very often, it is not *what* is written but *how* it is written.

People Books

These are, essentially, character-led books. As with all children's books there must also be a good story, but it is the characters that lead the story rather than the other way round. In other words, the story is secondary to the main point, whatever that may be. The problem with writing a people book is that so often the characters can take over and 'plot' goes out the window. The result is a wonderful character study but no framework in which those characters can be contained. I think the best people books start out with a situation and develop from there, but I'm not convinced you can set out to write a people book – I think they just happen.

Animal Stories

The *Animal Ark* series (and spin-offs) are probably the most successful examples of good animal stories that work. However, unless you're writing for the Picture Book market I would say that this is a hard area to get right. Most animal stories come across as too 'cutesy' – on the other hand, it's hard to make cuddly animals edgy! If you're dead set on writing about animals, my advice would be to combine your Animal Story with one of the other subject categories.

Taboo Areas

I would like to say that there are no taboo areas when writing children's fiction but that isn't true. What I can say is that the areas I consider to be taboo are probably not the ones you would expect.

I don't believe that there is any subject that is too 'adult' for children. Rape, incest, abuse, teenage pregnancies, drug addiction, homelessness, are all subjects that can, and should, be covered in children's fiction (though, of course, the age of the target readership has to be taken into account). Berlie Doherty's *Dear Nobody* deals with the issue of teenage pregnancy; Michelle Magorian's *Goodnight Mister Tom* deals with child abuse; Melvyn Burgess's *Junk* deals with drug abuse; Meg Rosoff's *How I Live Now* deals with anorexia, sex and self-harming. And these are all award-winning books – with good reason. They deal with the issues concerned with intelligence, insight and sensitivity.

So, technically, there is no subject matter that can't be covered in children's fiction. However, there are areas that I have allocated as my own personal 'taboos'.

Talk to any children's reader or editor and you will quickly discover that there are certain book ideas that crop up time and time again on the slush pile. I have seen hundreds of variations on the *Mr Men* books, *The Shoe People* (particularly tools and fruit coming to life), *Thomas the Tank Engine* (Desmond the Dustcart/Tommy the Tipper Truck etc.), *Fireman Sam* (the milkman is a popular alternative to the fireman) and *Animals of Farthing Wood*. Roald Dahl, Enid Blyton and Beatrix Potter imitators also crop up with alarming frequency. Recurring themes are: missing socks; supermarket trolleys coming to life; much-loved pets (particularly cats); foiled burglaries; tooth fairies; bathtime; bereavement; children being whisked up into the clouds during the night. An editor friend of mine's own personal favourite is *The Holocaust from a Hare's Point of View*. Mine is *Young Dung, the Story of a Dung Beetle*.

I could go on – but I won't. Suffice to say that these are 'taboo' areas as far as publishing is concerned.

Political Correctness

One particular book comes to my mind whenever the subject of political correctness rears its ugly head and that is *Abigail at the Beach* by Felix Pirani (now out of print).

Abigail at the Beach caused the most incredible furore when it was first published in 1988. It was even discussed in the House of Commons!

A Picture Book, it tells the story of Abigail, who visits the beach with her father. While Dad reads his book (assisted by three cans of beer), Abigail builds 'the biggest sandcastle in the world'. When her sandcastle is threatened by three boys, two girls and a dog, Abigail threatens to get her Dad to hang two of the boys upside down by their heels, to break the other boy's arms and to frazzle his bike and to shoot holes in the dog.

The book is cleverly and realistically written with a certain tongue-in-cheek, subversive humour. The objections, however, were vociferous and concerned both the beer drinking and the violence.

This, to my mind, is political correctness gone loony, with adults taking a totally unrealistic view of what children are really like and how they really behave. Have you ever made a visit to the playground of your local primary school at break-time? I assure you it is one of the most violent places on earth!

Other books, including many Enid Blyton 'classics', have been revised to conform with current thinking. Again quite rightly. Some of Enid Blyton's characterisation leaves a very unpleasant taste in my mouth. Although Enid Blyton's official biographer begs to differ. Writing in the *Daily Mail* recently, she comments, 'It can only be a matter of time before the stop-at-home, cake-baking mummies of Blyton's fiction will be sent out to work in shipyards as crane drivers while the daddies have to relinquish their City jobs and become house-husbands.'

It is true that some people get all hot and bothered at the mere mention of political correctness. 'The trouble with children's books today,' writers complain, 'is that they have to be so terribly PC. Don't they?'

Or, 'I used to love fairy stories when I was a child. But they're not allowed these days, are they?' Or, 'I've given my book a 'green' theme because I thought that would make it more PC.'

Let's examine those complaints. In my opinion, being politically correct means using a bit of common sense, being responsible. The only time you have deliberately to set out to write a politically correct book is when writing for the educational market, which has much more rigid requirements. Yet if, for example, we take the subject of schools, then books set in boarding schools will not have wide appeal – the large majority of the population could not afford to send their children to boarding school, even if they wanted to. Stories set in schools should, on the whole, be based in the state sector and must reflect a multi-cultural society – because that's the way it is.

On the other hand, beware of going too far. Just because we have equality of the sexes these days doesn't mean that you can *never* portray a woman washing up, or *never* portray a man mending a car. Children's writers have the freedom to create situations and form characters in whichever way they want – providing they reflect the situation of the population as a whole.

One of the problems with recreating traditional Fairy Tales for today's child is that Fairy Tales of the past haven't always been terribly politically correct. Before you all start groaning, here me out.

Most Fairy Tales are about boys, men and male adventures. When females do feature in the tales, they tend to play insignif-icant, passive roles, or are portrayed as evil, ugly schemers.

Loving, watching, serving or hatching evil are the main activities permitted to women in Fairy Tales.

There is little doubt that children learn a great deal about the world through stories, so what does this highly popular form of the story say about the role of women? That girls are not very important or positive characters? That females have less exciting, less varied, less independent and less intelligent lives than males?

I'm not suggesting for one minute that you start producing stories such as those featured in James Finn Garner's wonderful collection of *Politically Correct Bedtime Stories*. These were written, tongue-in-cheek, to make a point *against* 'sexist, racist, sizeist, ethnocentrist reading matter'. Finn Garner's version of 'Little (Vertically Challenged surely!) Red Riding Hood' has the resolute young feminist setting off to her grandmother's house with a basket of fresh fruit and mineral water 'not because this is women's work, mind you, but because the deed was generous and helped to engender a feeling of community'.

As you can probably tell, Finn Garner's deeply ironic and sophisticated stories are written for adults. Nevertheless, the last twenty years has seen the traditional Fairy Tale turned upside down. Helpless princesses, wicked stepmothers and triumphant (male) wolves have been replaced by more positive role models, and less predictable outcomes.

As far as giving a 'green' theme, or any other sort of PC theme, to a children's book is concerned, do be very careful. Remember that the story must come first and that children will be highly sceptical of any message that is forced upon them rather than growing naturally from the story.

Diversity

By 2010, one in every five children will be black or minority ethnic. 2006 saw the launch of a Diversity Matters conference (funded by the Arts Council England and organised by the Centre for Literacy in Primary Education) – this being the first in a number of initiatives aimed at promoting diversity in children's publishing.

What emerged from this conference was that children's literature is still far from sufficiently diverse, either in content or availability, to meet the needs of the children of the very diverse society that makes up twenty-first-century Britain. Publishing and bookselling remain largely white and middle-class and publishers are failing to reach out to other groups.

We are not only talking about multi-culturalism here. Diversity is about all groups in our society and other minority groups are similarly under-represented in children's writing. Children who are disabled, for example, children who have learning difficulties or who are gay.

As writers, this is heady stuff – your creative antennae should be twitching. As children's publishers properly wake up to this whole issue of diversity, there will be opportunities to fill the gap left by a paucity of good books in this area. For example, there is almost no tradition of special literature for children in the Arab world (other than imported titles) and a few writers are already responding to the challenge with titles such a *Kiss the Dust* by Elizabeth Laird, *Benny and Omar* by Eoin Colfer and *The Breadwinner* by Deborah Ellis. But there is a long way to go.

National Curriculum

This is another area that disturbs writers largely because they think that books must fit in with the National Curriculum and they haven't got a clue what that might involve.

I talked about the requirements of the National Curriculum and the Literacy Hour in Chapter Three so I won't add to it at this stage. My advice, when writing General Fiction, is to forget the National Curriculum. In all likelihood, the last thing children will want to do is read fiction based on a subject on which they've just completed a homework assignment!

IDEAS AND INSPIRATION

In my experience, writers tend to fall into two categories: those who have more ideas for stories than they know what to do with and yet can't put them down on paper, and those who find the writing part easy, yet are often struggling for inspiration.

Coming up with an idea is easy – it's just a question of turning every aspect of your day into a potential story. So take a deep breath and start by thinking what has happened to you so far today? Did the postman deliver a wrong letter to your address? Who was that woman who shook her fist at you as you crossed the road? And, this evening, did you really see lights in that boarded-up house next to the school?

Probably none of these things happened to you, but they are examples of everyday things that *could* have happened and could easily be turned into a book idea. Catherine MacPhail's inspiration for her first children's books came from a true, and terrible, event that happened to her daughter.

Catherine's daughter was being bullied at school and the bullying eventually culminated in her daughter being attacked by a gang of girls and dangled by her feet off a bridge over a busy road. The result of this incident was the writing of *Run Zan Run*, a book that went on to win the Kathleen Fidler Award. As Catherine herself has said, teasingly, to her daughter, 'It may be the worst thing that ever happened to you, pet – but it's the best thing that ever happened to me!'

If, like Catherine, you can get ideas from children themselves, you have the added advantage of knowing that what you have come up with is going to be of real interest. Another way of coming up with ideas is to scan newspapers and magazines. Newspapers and magazines can help focus the mind on what is 'real' for children today. 'For a children's book?' I hear you murmur. Yes, for a children's book. For many a workshop session, I have turned up laden with every conceivable tabloid newspaper and tacky magazine, which I have then thrown onto the floor, telling the group they have twenty minutes to come up with an idea. The results, often prompted by the most unlikely stories, have been quite spectacular. And Anne Fine's *Flour Babies* was prompted by her reading in the newspaper of a real-life experiment conducted in the States. A class of delinquent children had been given bags of flour to look after for a week and a prize went to the child who brought back their 'flour baby' in the best condition.

Another novel submitted to me was called *The Quiet Bride*. I found the title quite intriguing and was even more intrigued to find that the book was based on a true story that the author had found in the newspaper, *Orlando Sentinel*:

JILTED BRIDE WHO LIVED 35 YEARS IN GARDEN DIES
Reading, England – An English bride who lived in her garden for 35 years after being abandoned at the altar was found dead over the weekend. Joan Abery, 70, had refused to go back into her home after being spurned by her fiancé. She built herself a shelter from trees, twigs and brightly coloured umbrellas in the front garden of her home and furnished it with car seats and briefcases. She had left her house unchanged since the day the wedding should have taken place.

And if you're thinking you've heard this idea somewhere before (pure Miss Haversham surely!) then you'd be right – but so what? As I've already said, many people argue that there are only a finite number of plot lines in any case. It's the personal touch that you give to those plots that makes the difference.

Another way of keeping in touch with what children want and enjoy is by watching children's television. Children's programming (on terrestrial TV) runs from around 3.30PM until 6PM (if you include *Neighbours*), Monday to Friday. This will give you a good selection of programmes for all age groups and is a couple of hours well spent; it will accurately illustrate current fashions, trends and interests. So pour yourself a mug of tea, put your feet up and indulge in a well-deserved break in front of the television. And if anyone asks, say I said it was okay!

And it goes without saying that you should think about the children's books you enjoy and consider what it was that inspired them. Often this will give you a clue as to where to hunt for your own inspiration.

Remembering Ideas

Once you've got those ideas flowing thick and fast, you have to learn how to remember them and translate them into workable fiction concepts.

How often have you woken in the night after the most amazing dream and thought, 'I'll definitely remember it in the morning – and then woken the next morning with no clearer recollection than a faint niggling feeling about nothing in particular at the back of your mind? The only way to remember that dream is to sit straight up and *write it down*.

It's the same with ideas. When you have one, *write it down*. Not in a few hours' time, or the next day, or even the next time you think of it. Write it down *immediately*. Get into the habit of always having a pen and paper handy, even when you go to bed.

Once you have written down your ideas, you need to decide how you're going to store them. One solution is to have an 'ideas book' where you note down ideas as they come to you; sometimes, as already mentioned, ideas might come from a newspaper or magazine clipping, in which case it is better to cut out the item and keep it. I would suggest buying a box, or file, where you can keep both cuttings and the ideas book together. Review these regularly. If you're the highly organised type, you could invest in a card-index system and have all your ideas neatly categorised by subject; but remember that if you categorise an idea too rigidly at the start, you can inhibit its development later on.

Developing Ideas

Okay – you've got to the stage where you've had a few ideas and you've written them down. Now you need to start developing them. Sit down with your box or file and sift through the various thoughts you've had. Pick out one that really takes your fancy; different ideas will appeal at different times and there's no earthly point in struggling with an idea that you don't feel enthusiastic about – yet.

Now pose the question, '*What if?*' This opens up all sorts of possibilities.

Take the wrongly delivered letter I mentioned previously. *What if* you open it and discover that it contains a treasure map? *What if* it is a blackmail letter, not for you but for that nice boy who lives next door? *What if* it is addressed to someone who *used* to live next door but has long since been dead?

See what I mean? Already you have the beginnings of three different types of stories – an Adventure Story, a People Story and a Ghost Story.

Another method is brainstorming – this can be done either on your own or in a group. Write down your initial story idea in the middle of the page and draw a circle around it. Then let your imagination run riot. So turn to Page 102, let's take the word 'letter' and see where we get to.

I'll leave it up to you to come up with a story from the map. Bear in mind that it doesn't have to be centred round the idea with which you started – you may well find that one of your 'offshoots' provides you with most inspiration.

Ideas: Exercises

- Write a story based on the newspaper clipping from the *Orlando Sentinel*.
- Buy a tabloid newspaper and, after scanning its pages, develop a story idea from something you have read or seen in it.
- Apply the question 'What if?' to the initial idea and see what happens.

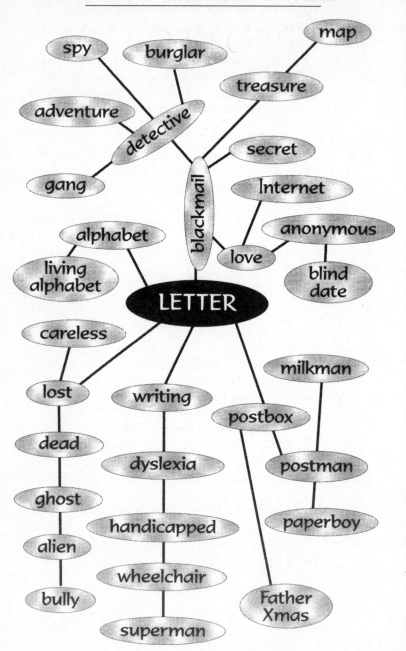

CHAPTER ELEVEN

PLOTTING

Some writers say that they have no idea what is going to happen in their story until they write it.

'A book just *happens*, doesn't it? I just go with the flow.'

While I wouldn't want to discourage such spontaneity, unless they are very experienced writers indeed they will often end up with a seemingly unconnected series of events with no discernible beginning, middle or end, and no structure on which to base other aspects of their story.

A book needs to be planned very carefully before the actual process of writing begins. This doesn't mean that change isn't possible once you have started to write. After all, half the fun of writing fiction is that characters become so real that they get up and speak and act for themselves. However, if you at least set off with some form of 'map', then you know where to take the detours and, most importantly, when to return to the main route once more.

In his book *Writing for Children and Teenagers*, Lee Wyndham describes plot as 'a plan of action devised to achieve a definite and much desired end – through cause and effect'.

Three by Three

Take this classic story outline:

> Boy meets girl.
> Boy loses girl.
> Boy gets girl.

What is implied in these three three-word sentences is that a story has a beginning, a middle and an end. Plot, at its most basic level, is rather like a three-legged bar stool. One leg represents the beginning, one the middle and one the end – if you lose just one of those legs the whole stool falls over. The same will happen with your story.

Although this very basic story structure won't work for more complicated stories, it is surprising how often it doees work, and how full these stories can be.

Here is Cinderella:

> Cinderella can't go.
> She attends anyway.
> Cinderella gets Prince.

And here is the Pied Piper:

> Man lures rats.
> People won't pay.
> Man takes children.

If you are working on a story at the moment, try applying this simple technique (and yes you are allowed to cheat by using apostrophes). When doing this exercise, try to use three different verbs as this will force you to consider the three parts of your story – what it is about, what happens and how it ends. Which is what I am going to talk about now.

Beginnings, Middles and Endings

As already discussed, the foundation plan of any story is a beginning, a middle and an ending. In order to weed out these three essential components, I would suggest that you answer three very basic questions. These are:

1 What is the story about?
2 What is the problem?
3 What happens?

What is the story about? You should be able to answer this question in one sentence. If you are struggling to answer the question in one sentence it is probably because you are trying to include several different story ideas within the one story. This isn't going to work when writing for children so it is important that you work hard on refining a very exact answer. So if we take three published stories, the three answers to question one above, might be:

1 The story is about a witch and her cat. (*Winnie the Witch* by Valerie Thomas and Korky Paul.)
2 The story is about a King who is very untidy. (*Cold Feet* by Susan Eames.)
3 The story is about a girl who is being bullied. (*Run Zan Run* by Catherine MacPhail.)

What is the problem? If we were to write stories based purely on each of the sentences above, we would, in all probability, come up with some fairly dreary texts. So as well as establishing the subject matter there also needs to be a 'problem'. It is this 'problem' that makes your main character finally take action in order to reach a certain goal and persuades the reader to keep turning the pages to find out 'what happens'. Bear in mind that the need to find a solution, or resolution, should be *crucial* – relative, of course, to the age group you are writing for.

So, for example, if we take the second example from above – *Cold Feet* – we have a story about a King who is very untidy. The 'problem' is that his wife, the Queen, has said that unless the King smartens up his act, she will no longer bake his favourite fruitcake for tea. In the context of this particular story, it is crucial that the King's problem is resolved.

In a children's book (and, in my opinion, in any book), it is important to get to the point of the story quickly. So let's take the first two examples above and see how quickly they get to the 'problem':

Winnie the Witch

Winnie the Witch lived in a black house in the forest. The house was black on the outside and black on the inside. The carpets were black. The chairs were black. The bed was black and it had black sheets and black blankets. Even the bath was black.

Winnie lived in her black house with her cat, Wilbur. He was black too. And that is how the trouble began.

And there we have it – the problem. Or a first hint at the problem anyway.

Cold Feet

Once upon a time, there were a King and Queen. Most of the time, they were terribly unhappy. The only trouble was that the King was terribly untidy – he would leave his clothes all over the palace.

'If you leave ANY more clothes lying around,' said the Queen one morning, as she picked up a jumper, some hats and a coat off the bedroom floor, 'or lose your socks again – I'll – I'll – I won't make any more special fruit cake for tea!'

And she stormed out.

And, again, there we have it – the problem.

What happens? This is a series of connected events preventing the cause from being resolved. In other words it is your plot. The 'problem' *will* be resolved but not, necessarily, in quite the way you might expect. It is important that effect isn't too predictable and that sufficient conflict is introduced.

By focusing your mind on these three basic headings, you will be able to create a story with a clear beginning, middle and end. By answering, 'What is the story about?' and, 'What is the problem?' the reader will know, very quickly, exactly what they are reading about and why. And so long as 'finding a resolution' is crucial, the reader will keep turning the pages to find out what happens. It is worth saying, as well, that each chapter, or section, should refer directly back to the original problem in order for the book to maintain its three-pronged structure.

THEME

In this new version of my book, I have deliberately demoted this whole area of 'theme' by mentioning it later in the chapter. In my opinion, children's writers, and in particular *new* children's writers, get far too hung up on this whole 'theme thing' and will often sacrifice any sort of plot for the sake of theme.

Theme should evolve naturally from the bare bones of your story – if you focus on it too obviously, you will be in danger of becoming didactic. Often the real theme to your book will only reveal itself when you have finished writing and some sort of basic truth is established. It is then that the reader will realise that as well as being a romping good adventure, the story was also about love/jealousy/revenge – or whatever theme you decide to focus on.

It is important to realise that not all children's books need to hold a deeper theme. Very often, particularly when writing Young Fiction, it would be ridiculous to try to pull a theme from the midst of what is essentially a light, entertaining and humorous tale.

THE MECHANICS OF PLOTTING

Once you have established the foundation plan of your storry – its 'three legs' – you can start to work on a more detailed plot.

A good plotting exercise is to think of an idea for a book of around 3000 words. Divide those words into between five and ten chapters and roughly plot out what is going to happen in each. This way you get the balance of your book right.

For example, the plot outline for *Jimmy Woods and the Big Bad Wolf* by Mick Gowar (now out of print but it doesn't matter as the principles remain the same) may have looked like this:

1 Jimmy Woods picks on hero as he makes his way to sweet shop. Steals his sweet money.

2 Hero takes his dog, Prince, to the shops and Prince scares off a terrified Jimmy Woods – for now.

3 Jimmy Woods is spotted by hero paying a visit to Granny Timpson's house. Hero is worried and decides to check up on Granny Timpson.

4 Granny Timpson won't let Hero into her house. Hero's sister, Debbie, persuades her to let her in.

5 Hero is allowed in as well. Discovers that Jimmy Woods is terrorising Granny Timpson and stealing from her.

6 Hero and Debbie put a plan into action. Involves sitting Prince in chair in dark room with rug over him to make him look like Granny. Prince goes for Jimmy Woods and chases him off – for good this time.

7 Story of how Jimmy Woods was scared off by a 'wolf' gets around but no one believes him. He is a laughing stock and no longer a threat.

The story is about a bully called Jimmy Woods and the problem is that not only is he picking on our hero but, more seriously, is threatening a poor, vulnerable old lady as well. Every chapter is relevant to, and advances, the 'problem'. It inevitably works its way towards resolution, but the tension is maintained by constantly introducing new elements to the story.

The story itself, though, is worked through logically, with approximately two 'events' in each chapter, and neither 'accident' nor 'coincidence' play any part in the plotting plan. This helps sustain the credibility of the story. If you are tempted (or forced!) to use coincidence as a way of resolving your story, look again at the plot – it is usually a sign of weakness on the writer's part. It's what I call 'and then he woke up and found it was all a dream'-type stories. To me it always reeks of an author having run out of ideas to extricate their protagonist from the plot. It's like 'and then the fairy godmother waved her magic wand and made everything okay', or 'and then the police turned up and threw all the baddies in prison'.

Note, also, that factual happenings *only* have been used in the plotting plan. This is crucial. Many other details will, of course, be included in this story as it progresses, but it is worth remembering that character analysis and background detail are not 'plot'. In children's fiction, they make the plot seem more interesting; they do not in themselves advance the story.

Catherine's Plan

Catherine MacPhail won the (then) Kathleen Fidler Award with her book *Run Zan Run*. She uses her own special formula for plotting out her books, which, with her permission, I am now going to share with you.

She begins by working out, roughly, how many chapters she is going to have in her book. *Run Zan Run* is between 20–25,000 words; Catherine would have known that it was going to be roughly this length before she started writing because it was specified in the Award rules. So, once she had her idea, she decided that sixteen chapters was going to be a feasible length, ensuring chapters were neither too long nor too short.

She then writes down the following headings:

1 What is the problem?
2 Build on the problem
3 Open out the plot ...
4–12 Filler
13 Crescendo
14 Nothing Can Save Her Now!
15 Baddies get done in
16 Tidy up

Let's run through this plan and see how it applied to *Run Zan Run*, the book Catherine ended up writing.

What is the Problem?

Katie is being mercilessly bullied by Ivy Toner and her cronies:

> Everyone told her one day Ivy Toner would grow tired of picking on her, move on to fresher, more fearing ground.
> But when? It had been months since it began ...

This is the problem. It is what the book is about. Katie is being bullied by a gang of girls to such an extent that the reader feels they could even threaten her life. Obviously, it is *crucial* to Katie that this problem – this cause – is resolved. And if it is crucial to Katie, it is crucial to the reader.

Build on the Problem

Once the basic problem has been set up, we need to explore it in more detail.

By the end of Chapter One, Zan, the mysterious girl who lives in a cardboard box on the dump, has been introduced. In Chapter Two, her role becomes more important as we see her starting to befriend Katie and side with her against the evil Ivy:

> The girl stepped from the darkness. Zan. Her face dirty and her hair matted, but her eyes bright and challenging.
>
> 'You again . . .' Ivy's voice trembled. She was afraid. Ivy Toner was afraid!

Some background detail is also built into this chapter – not in one big chunk but gradually as, piece by piece, we learn the finer details of Katie's life. Such as what her parents are like and her relationship with them:

> 'Is something bothering you, Katie?' Her mother sat across from her. She was very pretty with large dark eyes and a head of rich dark curls. She looked much younger than her forty-four years.

Or details about where Katie lives:

> Zan held back, looking at the house. How inviting it must seem to her, Katie thought. The warm glow of the lamps lighting the windows, the hall lit up and the red carpeted stairs rising to the floor above. There were sounds too, music and laughter. Her parents' party in full progress. Katie wanted her to come in so much.

Open Out the Plot

Obviously, the fact that Katie is being bullied isn't alone sufficient to sustain a book of this length. Other factors need to be
developed to give the plot depth and interest.

This added depth is provided by Zan, who is appalled at the
fact that Katie has told everyone about her:

> 'They're everywhere,' Zan went on breathlessly. 'Police,
> social workers, do-gooders. I wanted to stay here for a
> while. I like this town, it's big enough to hide in, but not to
> get lost in . . . Now I can't – because of you – I helped you.
> I've never helped anyone in my life . . . and this is how you
> thank me.'

Katie is forced into a position of having to lie about Zan. She
tells everyone that she made her up and everyone believes her,
even Ivy's two cronies. Their own theory about Zan is that she
was really Katie in disguise. Everyone believes Katie – except for
Ivy, and Ivy is going to prove that Zan exists even if it takes to
the end of her days.

Filler

The middle part of the book contains the bulk of the plot – the
effect – what Catherine MacPhail calls the *Filler*.

It's hard to be specific about exactly how *you* should fill your
book without knowing the specific story you want to write.
Read *Run Zan Run* to see how Catherine did it. Think about
how your baddie prevents your hero from resolving the initial
problem; consider what actions your hero takes to overcome
these obstacles. One difficulty should constantly lead to another
right the way through until the resolution.

Ask yourself the following as you finish each and every
chapter: 'Has this chapter, in some way, addressed the initial
problem established in Chapter One?' Be honest with yourself –
if your text has strayed from the main route, there is a danger that
your reader will get lost.

Crescendo

Towards the end of the book, there should be a 'plateau of awfulness'. This is where the tension builds and everything that *can* go wrong *does* go wrong. Various strands of the plot begin to be pulled together, but resolution still seems as far away as ever.

In *Run Zan Run*, this point comes in Chapter Thirteen when we discover Zan's terrible secret – the reason why her existence must never be discovered. She believes she is suspected of causing a fire in her parent's home in which they both died. We learn who the real killer is as the plot reaches its crescendo:

> 'I saw him, Katie ... the man who did burn the house down. And he saw me. He said he'd get me one day ... I've been running ever since.'

Nothing Can Save Her Now!

Just as we think nothing can get any worse, the plot spirals out of control into a final 'black' moment. In *Run Zan Run*, the killer has cornered Zan and Ivy Toner finally gets Katie on her own, without Zan to help her.

> No one knew where she was. No one knew Zan existed. It was hopeless praying for help. Nothing could save her now!

Baddies Get Done In

In all children's books, 'good' somehow has to triumph over 'bad'. This won't necessarily mean that the 'baddies get done in', but it will mean that the 'goodies' come out on top.

In *Run Zan Run*, the cavalry arrive at the last minute in the shape of Katie's teacher, her Mum and Dad, and two policemen. Katie is rescued from Ivy, and Zan from the killer. The truth dawns and everyone sees Ivy for what she really is – a stupid, but nonetheless evil, bully.

Tidy Up

The last chapter is there to tidy up any loose ends. It should be brief and to the point. If you do feel a need to go on at length it may mean you have a weak link in your plot, an aspect that has not been resolved as a consequence of events. This final chapter should also underline the 'basic truth' of your book – the theme, or message.

Catherine's final chapter is barely four pages, yet it tells us everything we need to know:

> 'I'd like to propose a toast,' her father said, and he held his glass high. 'To Katie and Zan ...' He smiled at each of them. 'Friends for ever.'

Plotting: Exercises

- Choose a children's book that you like (not a Picture Book or very young Reader) and apply the 'three-pronged bar-stool' approach.
- Think of a book idea of your own, sum up what it is *about* and what is the problem. Try to narrow this down to a couple of sentences.
- Take Catherine's Plan and work out how it could apply to your own book.

Obviously, your own personal plan may vary a little according to the sort of book you are writing. But if you adapt the bare bones of Catherine's plan to your needs, you won't go far wrong, whoever you are writing for.

CHAPTER TWELVE

CHARACTERISATION

Characterisation makes your story come alive. However strong your plot, without good characterisation you will have an uninvolving, superficial text on your hands: at best boring, at worst, dead.

Take those classics of children's literature, *Winnie the Pooh* and *The House at Pooh Corner*. They don't have the most exciting plots in the world. But combined with exquisitely drawn characters, the story becomes compulsive reading for young and old alike.

ANIMAL CHARACTERS

One of the reasons A. A. Milne's characters are so brilliant is that their individual characteristics are entirely human. As a group, the characters in *Pooh* form a typical community in which any one of us might live. There's an Eeyore in every street – the gloomy pessimist, always looking on the dark side. And a happy-go-lucky Pooh, who 'hasn't much brain but never comes to any harm'. And an Owl, who 'hasn't exactly got a brain, but he Knows Things'. And a scheming Rabbit, who 'hasn't learnt in books but can always think of a Clever Plan'.

A. A. Milne's writing demonstrates that, even when we're writing about animals, characterisation is every bit as important as it is when we're writing about human beings. I once attended a children's writing workshop and one of the students was writing a story about a cat – but the story wasn't working because none of us really *believed* in the cat. Then someone suggested that the cat reminded him of the woman who does the wine slot on a food-and-drink television programme (I name no names!). By the time of the next workshop session, the writer concerned had incorporated the woman's very specific characterisations into her cat. The cat sprang to life in front of our eyes – or ears! She became real: we could see her, hear her, feel her, almost touch her.

So if you are having trouble with your animal characters – if you feel that you have just another squirrel on your hands, or just another rabbit – base them on someone you know. The character will then become real in your mind and, as a result, real to your reader.

Sometimes, of course, it can work the other way around – i.e. an author may use an animal to describe a human being. For example, take this description of Edmond when Daisy meets him for the very first time in Meg Rosoff's *How I Live Now*:

> Now let me tell you what he looks like before I forget because it's not exactly what you'd expect from your average fourteen-year-old what with the CIGARETTE and hair that looked like he cut it himself with a hatchet in the dead of night, but aside from that he's exactly like some kind of mutt, you know the ones you see at the dog shelter who are kind of hopeful and sweet and put their nose straight into your hand when they meet you with a certain kind of dignity and you know from that second that you're going to take him home? Well that's him.

> Reader, I give you . . . Edmond!

HUMAN CHARACTERS

Human characters often present more problems. Many writers find that, while they are clear about their less detailed subsidiary characters, their main character refuses to develop beyond a one-dimensional cardboard cut-out. I think this is because our main character is often ourselves; it is the character we can identify with, the one from whose viewpoint the story is told. And, as in life, we can see the people around us by looking outwards, but to see ourselves we need a mirror.

For this reason, many writers find it helpful to develop their main character while studying a photograph or drawing. Don't feel ashamed about this; it doesn't mean that you have no imagination, it just means that you are identifying with your main character to such an extent that it is impossible to be completely objective.

As I said earlier, a character can sometimes be created by a newspaper or magazine feature, or photograph. In my files, I have a large newspaper photograph of a young teenager sitting in the driving seat of a car, with a cigarette hanging out of his mouth and a black woolly cap pulled down over a white, pinched face. One day, I will write about that boy – and I will need that picture to keep him alive.

School photographs can be useful. All those rows and rows of children staring at the camera – that one, third from the right in the second row – he's got a look about him. What was he like? Why is the boy next but one to him glancing across at him?

When I was working for teenage magazines, we used to employ young models and actors to act out the photostories. The writers all kept details of these young people, including their photographs. These proved vital when coming up with new storylines on a weekly basis; often a photograph alone would be enough to spark off an idea.

However, it would be a mistake to think that the best way of conveying a character, any character, is by describing them in photographic detail. Sometimes a better impression of a character can be given by focusing on just one part of their body, or dress or on something that they do, or are doing. Take this passage from *Junk* by Melvin Burgess where we meet Lily for the first time:

> She was dancing. I mean she was doing things and dancing at the same time. She'd go and put on a new cassette, or find a better track on the old one or just look through what was there, then she'd go over and pinch a fag or a joint off someone, or tidy up fag ends or paper cups or something . . . and all the time she was moving to the music, dancing,

swaying her head, just really going with the music. She just couldn't stand still. She was smiling all the time, not at anyone, just to herself and the good time she was having. Her mouth was even wider than mine and her eyes turned into two, black, happy little gaps in her face when she smiled. She was beautiful.

By the end of this passage, we know nothing about the way Lily looks except that she has a wide mouth and black eyes. Yet I can see her . . . and I *know*, without knowing anything else about her, that she *is* beautiful.

But it isn't just the look of someone that brings a character to life. Smell, sound, feel, likes and dislikes are all part of a person as well. Have you noticed, for example, how often characters in children's fiction are portrayed as liking a particular food? Popeye was mad about spinach; Paddington Bear's staple diet was marmalade just as Pooh's was honey.

Children's author Philip Ridley knows this better than anyone. In his book *Krindlekrax*, Ruskin's mum can't live without teabags and toast. In *Kasper in the Glitter*, Kasper is an expert at making Banoffi pie because he knows that it cheers his mum up:

Banoffi is one of the most delicious pies ever invented. It's made with sliced bananas, gooey toffee, and topped off with coffee-flavoured cream, chocolate granules, and a large dollop of marmalade.

The marmalade, to be honest, is Kasper's own particular addition to the recipe. He says it gives the dish a much-needed twang. And he should know. After all, nobody could have made as many Banoffi pies as ten-year-old Kasper Whisky.

Note the detail that Philip gives to this description. He gets right inside Kasper's head by describing something as inconsequential as how to make a Banoffi pie. Food is something all of us can relate to – it elicits an immediate emotional response in adults and children alike.

Philip Ridley also uses nicknames to reinforce his characters. In *The Meteorite Spoon*, Filly and Fergal call each other Sis and

Brov; in *Krindlekrax*, the school caretaker is called Corky. This happens in real life, so why not in books? It's yet another technique to make your characters seem more tangible, more real – more like the child reading about them.

So before sitting down to write your story, I suggest that you write a complete separate profile of your main character, for your reference only. Think about the foods that your character likes; hobbies; friends; what he or she sounds like; smells like; the look of the skin on his face; how often she has to wash her hair – *everything*, and *anything*, you can think of. I once asked some students to think of a person they knew and write down two things that best summed them up. One lady was a teacher and the character she wrote about was a boy in her class. The two characteristics she assigned him were 'squelchy armpits' and 'the smell of plasticine'. I never met him, but I can see that child to this day!

One final tip (for the very lazy) on bringing your main character to life; buy a book on star signs. I have a wonderful book called *Heaven on Earth* by Fritz Wegner: it certainly isn't a book for the astrological expert, but for my purposes it is unrivalled.

Let's take a fictional character, Lucy, born on 25 March. My book immediately tells me she's an Arian, which is the sign of the ram. It also tells me that her likes are 'anything new, fast, fun, thrilling or competitive'. In action she is 'swift and intrepid. Has a direct manner and clear-cut views; remarks are candid and often satirical. Is determined, and does not take kindly to being thwarted'. At best she is 'enthusiastic, courageous, carefree, amicable, exciting, decisive, straightforward, quick-witted and energetic.' At worst she is 'headstrong, irresponsible, vain, hot-tempered, aggressive, ruthless, reckless, tactless and egotistical'.

It tells me a whole host of other things as well, including her favourite gemstones, the sort of people she gets on with and what she's like at school. Maybe Fritz Wegner should write a children's book . . .

SUBSIDIARY CHARACTERS

Don't forget that your main character isn't the only character in your book. Subsidiary characters can be just as important to the story, but too often they come across as nothing more than shadows.

The number of characters you should include in your story depends upon the length of the book and, therefore, the age group you are writing for. Generally speaking, the younger the age group, and the shorter the book, the fewer characters you should have. In many Picture Books, there are often only one or two characters. *Rosie's Walk* by Pat Hutchins has a hen and a fox: *Winnie the Witch* by Valerie Thomas and Korky Paul, a witch and her cat. This is because, in Picture Books, situations are as important as the characters and simplicity is vital. But the older the age group, the more important the characters become, and the more characters and complexity you will need to include.

Subsidiary characters often provide the opportunity for a subplot. In a very serious story, they can provide opportunities for light relief. They are also good 'sounding boards' for the main character – through conversations with a subsidiary character the reader can learn how the main character is really feeling.

Remember, too, that no one character exists in isolation from another. The way that characters interact with each other tell us more about them, as people, than anything that they do. Body language can be just as telling as words.

Take this following passage from *Stone Cold* by Robert Swindells:

She came over. Every eye in the place followed her. She nodded at one of the three empty chairs. 'Anyone sitting here?' She sounded Scottish. I shook my head.

'Mind if I join you then?' I nodded, saying nothing. Being the New Me. She unslung her pack, dropped it next to mine and sat down. I lifted my mug and sipped tepid coffee, gazing out of the window.

She inserted her straw in her Coke and sucked. When I risked a glance at her she dropped her eyes. I sipped more coffee, sensing her eyes on my face. I mean I could actually feel them, like lasers.

The attraction between the two is almost palpable. It is far more intense than if the author had written about her falling into his arms. This is how young people *really* behave when they fancy each other. They size each other up, glance at each other and then look away, feel self-conscious, act cool. We've all been there so use your own experiences.

Stereotyping

There is a danger, when coming up with characters for a story, of falling into the trap of stereotyping: your baddie is unshaven and wearing a dirty raincoat, even though you know perfectly well that the most dangerous psychopaths are immaculately dressed and baby-faced; Granny is grey-haired and sitting in a rocking chair knitting booties, even though your own granny dresses in leathers and rides a motorbike.

Try, whenever possible, to turn the expected into the unexpected. Think of the stereotype – then write about the opposite. Many popular stories are based around role reversal – Kaye Umansky's *Romantic Giant*, whose title speaks for itself; Dick King-Smith's *The Sheep-Pig*, the story of a pig who thinks he's a sheep; and *Prince Cinders* and *Princess Smartypants*, both role-reversal stories by Babette Cole. One of my favourites was *Crummy Mummy and Me* by Anne Fine. This is a collection of stories about an outrageously irresponsible Mum, her slightly more responsible punk boyfriend, and Mum's ever-sensible and practical daughter, Mina. The following passage is a conversation between Mum and Mina at bedtime:

> MINA: I really think I ought to be going up to bed now.
> MUM: (*astonished*) Why?
> MINA: (*patiently*) Because it's getting rather late.
> MUM: It's not *that* late.
> MINA: (*looking at her watch*) It's well past my bedtime.
> MUM: Oh, you're getting older all the time. You don't need that much sleep.
> MINA: I do. Look at me. I've already got great big grey bags under my eyes.
> MUM: That's just the light.
> MINA: No it isn't.
> MUM: Well, what about this board game? Surely you can stay long enough to finish the *game*? It's nearly over.

MINA: It's nowhere near over. It'll take *ages*.

MUM: Oh, all *right*. Go on, then. I'll come up in a little while and tuck you in.

MINA: (*really relieved*) Oh, good, Mum. Thanks.

Role reversal at its best and funniest. And this passage brings me neatly onto the final, and most important, element of characterisation – dialogue.

DIALOGUE AND CHARACTERISATION

You can tell a lot about a person from the way that they speak. A shy person may stammer on certain words; someone who is not very sure of themselves may speak in short, unfinished sentences. A very confident person may constantly interrupt, cutting other people short.

In Philip Ridley's *Krindlekrax*, Ruskin Bond's mum, Wendy, says 'Polly-wolly-doodle-all-the-day' whenever she gets flustered. Ruskin's Dad, on the other hand, is always saying, 'It's not my fault.' Both these phrases, when used in dialogue, convey the characters of the users far better than any detailed description of the way they look and how they behave.

When writing dialogue, it is important to *sum up* the character of the particular person you are writing about and style their speech accordingly. The reader should be able to tell who is speaking without being told – *just* from the way the dialogue is written.

Take this dialogue from *The House at Pooh Corner*:

'I don't know how it is, Christopher Robin, but what with all this snow and one thing and another, not to mention icicles and such-like, it isn't so Hot in my field about three o'clock in the morning as some people think it is. It isn't Close, if you know what I mean – not so as to be uncomfortable. It isn't Stuffy. In fact, Christopher Robin, he went on in a loud whisper, 'Quite-between-ourselves-and-don't-tell-anybody, it's Cold.'

It's Eeyore speaking. It couldn't be anyone else – his dialogue *sums up* everything we know about him: his lugubriousness, his pessimism.

Dialect is another factor to consider when writing dialogue. The trick is to convey an accent, complete with all its mannerisms and oddities, while making it intelligible.

The following examples are from *Run Zan Run* by Catherine MacPhail:

> 'There's no' anywhere you can hide here, hen.'
> 'You gonny make me?'
> 'She fairly scared the knickers off you anyway.'
> 'You jist tell her to stay away from me.'

Note the words Cathy uses – *hen, gonny, jist* – all characteristic of the Scottish idiom. She thus helps to establish not only the background of her characters, but also a strong sense of place. And for the reader, the unfamiliar yet recognisable words provide a rich and colourful reading experience.

The way your character speaks must fit in with the type of book that you are writing. Just as if a story is set in Scotland, you must convey a Scottish accent, so if a story is set in the past your dialogue must give a flavour of those times. For this reason, if you don't feel confident about writing dialogue, make sure that you set your story in a time and region familiar to you.

Even so it is vital that your dialogue is realistic, so do listen to how people speak – and, in particular, how children speak: how they speak *today*, not how they spoke when you were a child.

'Children swear a lot today. Is it all right to have swearing in my book?' is a question I often get asked. It's hard to answer this one. Gratuitous swearing is not allowed but swearing that fits with the style of your story is acceptable in most fiction for older children. If you *are* using swear words, or any form of slang, do make sure that the words you use are up-to-date. At the time of writing, the word *cool* has come in, gone out and come in again. In the 1990s, many children use/have used unexpected adjectives such as *wizard* and *bad* to bestow praise – but these have now fallen from favour. It's impossible to stay ahead of the fashion, so try to keep your dialogue as timeless as possible.

We'll talk more about dialogue in the following two chapters: how to write it, how to use it to move the plot forward and how to achieve the correct balance of dialogue and narrative.

CHARACTER DEVELOPMENT

'Character Development' means just that – the characters in your book have to develop. If your main character is weak and silly at the beginning of your story and is still weak and silly at the end, what was the point of us reading your book. 'For the plot', I hear you say. 'To find out what happened.' Fine, but to read a book for plot alone isn't enough. Your characters have to move with the plot, they have to be affected in some way by the plot, and, as a result of what happens in the plot, they have to have changed in some way by the end – for better, or just occasionally in the case of subsidiary characters, for worse.

This is, after all, what happens in real life. The way in which we react to different situations determines who we are as people. Whether child or adult we don't stand still. Depending upon what happens to us we develop, we learn, we move on – that process is happening every day and it never stops. In the same way, characters that we create in fiction have to learn from the situations in which they are placed.

In Anne Fine's *Flour Babies*, Simon Martin learns that he isn't trapped in some sort of predestined downward spiral but is free to make his own decisions:

Louder and louder he sang. He wasn't trapped. He would be punished, but he wasn't trapped. And there'd be time enough to be responsible.

In Catherine MacPhail's *Run Zan Run*, Katie and Zan learn to trust other people and learn the truth of the saying 'united we stand' first hand:

Her mother joined in hugging Zan too, and Katie, never one to be left out, just held on tight. She could feel Zan shaking, the fear still upon her, and she could feel that fear abate, as her father's strength, her family's strength, comforted her.

Even Robert Swindells' *Stone Cold*, which can hardly be said to have a happy ending, ends on a positive note. Talking about homelessness, the main character writes:

> There has to be an end to this. I just hope it happens while I'm still around.

But perhaps the most dramatic illustration of character development is to be found in *Junk* by Melvin Burgess. This is, essentially, a love story, but it is also a shocking portrayal of drug abuse and the degradation of the human spirit. The book has a wide cast of characters, all of whom develop continually throughout the story. The two main characters, Tar and Gemma, learn something positive from their experience but this is far from the case for all of the characters involved in the story. For example, this next extract is the last we hear from Tar's Dad:

> One day, my boy, all this will be yours. As they say. All my goods and shackles, such as they are. There's no one else. The other thing you leave your children is your life – the example of it. One day, my boy . . .
>
> And so, in your absense, David, I raise my glass to you – a cup of tea actually – and I say, Here's to you. Good luck! Make the most of it.
>
> And don't end up like me.

Junk also teaches us a lot about creating characters with whom, although not necessarily sympathetic or likeable, we can identify. This is important. If a character is downright unpleasant from start to finish, we won't want to read about him or her. Gemma in *Junk* is a far from likeable character yet, despite everything, we can identify with her, we can sympathise with her, we care about her. This is because she has two sides to her – she is strong and assertive, but she is also weak and vulnerable. It is a question of creating rounded characters. No one is all bad, or all good; people are a mixture of the two, usually weighted one way or the other. That is how your characters should be in your book – real, rounded people, not just cardboard cut-outs.

Characterisation: Exercises

- Find an old school photo and, choosing a person you do like, and a person you don't like, list three small things that sum up each person.
- Bearing in mind the excerpt from *Crummy Mummy and Me,* invent a dialogue between two people trying to get across their individual characteristics in the way that they speak.

CHAPTER THIRTEEN

VIEWPOINT

Viewpoint is the *position* from which a story is told. It is rather like the camera position chosen by a film director and, as the director, you the writer have two decisions to make before you start filming. One is to decide *whose* viewpoint you are using; the other is to decide *which*.

WHOSE VIEWPOINT?

When writing for children, the main viewpoint character usually has to be a child. There are exceptions to this rule, particularly in books for younger children, but, even then, the viewpoint character is usually a child 'substitute' – i.e. to all intents and purposes, he or she *is* a child in an adult body. For example, *The Romantic Giant* by Kaye Umansky doesn't contain any child characters; the main viewpoint character is Waldo the giant. However, Waldo possesses an innocence and naivety that children are able to relate to.

It is the same with animal characters. Even if your main viewpoint character is not, technically, a young 'child' animal, he or she must possess qualities to which a child can relate. It is the quality of innocence that matters. I don't know what age Pooh is; or Mole in *The Wind in the Willows*. They are, in many ways, ageless. Both characters sometimes seem very old and wise, yet at other times they seem childlike and innocent. It is the innocence that appeals to the reading child.

Your viewpoint character must also be the same age, or preferably slightly older, than your target reader. Children like to feel
'grown-up' when they are reading and think it is 'babyish' to read
about someone younger than they are. They want to be a little older,
more mature, more powerful, than they are in reality – just as adults
like to read about characters who are an idealised version of themselves. So if your book is targeted at the 8–12 age range, your
viewpoint character ideally needs to be 12+. If it is a book essentially for the younger end of that age span, then 12 is fine. If it is
really a story more suited to the older end then you will probably
have to add a couple of years; for example, Katie, in *Run Zan Run*,
is nearly fourteen. You don't need, necessarily, to be specific about
the age of your viewpoint character; but you do need to think carefully about what stage of maturity your character has reached, so that
you are clear about his or her experience and capabilities. It is no
good writing a book for very young children that shows your viewpoint character walking to school on their own, or being at home
on their own. Similarly, if you are writing a school story, you need
to think about the level that your viewpoint character has reached.
Are they at primary school? If so, is it upper or lower, junior or
middle? Or have they moved on to secondary school?

When you've decided upon your viewpoint character's
approximate age, draw up a plan taking all aspects of their life
into account: where they live, how they dress, what they eat,
what music they listen to and so on. You need to inhabit that
character's viewpoint before you can write about it.

WHICH VIEWPOINT?

In modern children's books, the story is usually told through the
eyes (and other senses) of one 'viewpoint character'. Up to a
dozen different types of viewpoint are available to the children's
writer but, in practice, only a few are regularly used. Let's run
through the four basic choices with examples.

First Person
A story written in the first person is told from the point of view
of the narrator. This person is the character the reader is going
to identify with and appears as 'I' in the text.

> It all began last January, on a dark evening that was full of sleet. Funny, it's not long ago. I was just a kid then. But today is October 2nd, and this is where I begin to write, where I open a door into the past.
>
> (From *Dear Nobody* by Berlie Doherty)

At first glance, it would seem that this is an easy viewpoint choice to handle. No problems with making the main character come alive – because we are, straight away, inside the main character's head.

However, first person does have its drawbacks. It is an introspective style of writing and doesn't really work when there is a lot of action involved. Also, unless skilfully handled, it can become monotonous.

Generally speaking, it is a better choice when writing for older children and teenagers, as this type of story tends to rely more on introspection in any case.

Third Person Singular

This is the most popular viewpoint when writing for children. In my opinion, it is the easiest to handle and the most effective. The story is told in the third person (he, she or it) but from a single point of view only.

Nothing can be described that is not *directly experienced* by your viewpoint character. It is as if you, the writer, are sitting on his or her shoulder and seeing events from there *only*. You can know what your viewpoint character is feeling, but can only surmise what other characters are feeling from the way they look, behave and talk.

> The two figures were silent for several seconds. They then drifted away and spoke together, though Will could hear nothing of what they said.
>
> Finally they came close again, and he heard:
>
> 'Very well. You are making a mistake, though you give us no choice. We shall help you find this child.'
>
> (From *The Amber Spyglass* by Philip Pullman)

Note the phrase 'Will could hear nothing of what they said'.

Although this is written in the third person, we still only experience everything through Will's eyes and ears alone.

This viewpoint choice gives you all the advantages of strong reader identification with your main character, yet still leaves plenty of opportunity for descriptive narrative.

Third Person Plural or Multiple Viewpoint

This is where the story is told from no one particular viewpoint – the viewpoint shifts from person to person. Personally, I don't think this is a choice any new writer should be considering, although a number of established children's authors do use multiple viewpoint. It does give a certain amount of flexibility, in that it is easy to move from location to location, but it certainly doesn't help reader identification.

Enid Blyton used this viewpoint very successfully, but her books were largely plot-led with very little time spent exploring the emotions of her characters. A more recent notable example of multiple viewpoint is *Madame Doubtfire* by Anne Fine:

> All the way up the stairs, the children fought not to carry the envelope. Towards the top, Lydia took advantage of her height to force it down Christopher's jumper. Christopher pulled it out and tried to thrust it into Natalie's hand.
>
> 'Here, Natty,' he said. 'Give this to Dad.'
>
> Natalie shook her head so violently her hair whipped her cheeks pink. She interlaced her fingers behind her back. So Christopher tucked the envelope down the top of her pinafore dress, behind the yellow felt ducklings. Natalie's eyes filled with tears, and by the time Daniel Hilliard opened the door to let his children in, she was weeping gently.

It is as if all the characters are being observed equally minutely by an all-knowing outsider looking down on them. This is multiple viewpoint.

Narrator Viewpoint

The most famous example of this type of viewpoint is the *Just So Stories* by Rudyard Kipling, where the author breaks away from his story to acknowledge his reader as 'Dearly Beloved'. A. A. Milne opens *Winnie the Pooh* using narrator viewpoint, as does C. S. Lewis in *The Chronicles of Narnia*:

> This is the story of something that happened long ago when your grandfather was a child. It is a very important story because it shows how all the comings and goings between our world and the land of Narnia first began.

This is a traditional, formal storytelling technique that isn't often used nowadays as it can sound rather studied and old-fashioned.

How to Choose

Sometimes it is obvious, even before the planning stage, which viewpoint type you are going to have to use for your story. It depends what sort of story you have decided to write. At other times, however, you may be faced with a dilemma.

The most common confusion usually arises over whether to use first person or third person singular. There is no easy answer. Sometimes it helps to start writing and discover for yourself which viewpoint comes most naturally to you.

Don't forget, though, that third person singular can be remarkably close to first person – particularly if you give voice to your main character's thoughts. When I was thinking about writing this chapter on viewpoint, I remembered a book called *What About It Sharon?* by John Harvey, now sadly out of print. I was absolutely certain that this book would make an excellent example of the first person viewpoint. However, when I actually dug it out and re-read it, I realised that it isn't written in the first person at all, but third person singular:

> Debbie Bradley was a right bitch. A right little bitch! Walking round town with him like that. Strutting across from the fountain to the bus station on those stupid high heels of hers. It's pity she didn't fall flat on her face, like the time she did when they went up to London on that visit.

The only clue we have that it isn't written in the first person is 'when *they* went up to London', which tells us we are not reading about personal experience.

Very generally speaking (there are no hard-and-fast rules when it comes to creative writing), I would suggest using third person singular for the more action-based story for the younger reader, and first person, perhaps, for the more introspective, character-led novel for the older reader. What I would *not* suggest doing is switching backwards and forwards between a number of different viewpoints simultaneously. Take the following snatch of dialogue:

'Have a good day at school, did we?' said Mrs Moore, thinking, not for the first time, how pretty her daughter would look if only she would smile more often.

'Not particularly,' said Debbie, slamming the front door behind her. She wondered why her mother couldn't make a perfectly simple enquiry without sounding sarcastic.

Mrs Moore sighed and turned back to the kitchen, leaving Debbie to sort herself out. She knew she'd only get even more angry otherwise. Debbie would leave her things strewn all over the hall, and guess who'd have to tidy it up later on?

Debbie fought back tears of frustration as she watched her mother's departing back. Her mother just wasn't interested in her.

'Tea's ready in half an hour,' said Mrs Moore.

That'd take the wind out of her sails. Usually, she made Debbie get her own tea, but that extra half-hour would give her time. She glanced towards the half-empty bottle of gin on the kitchen side.

'Oh, see if I care!' she heard Debbie shout from the hall, followed by the familiar stamping of feet up the stairs.

This passage would work much better if written from one viewpoint only. As this is an excerpt from a children's story, the viewpoint character will have to be Debbie:

'Have a good day at school, did we?' said Debbie's Mum.

'Not particularly,' said Debbie, the welcoming smile she'd been going to give her mother freezing on her lips.

She slammed the door behind her and wondered, not for the first time, why her mother couldn't make a perfectly simple enquiry without sounding sarcastic.

'Mum . . .' she began, but her mother just sighed and went back into the kitchen.

Debbie hurled her things angrily across the hall floor, tears of disappointment and frustration stinging her eyes. Her mother just wasn't interested in her. All she cared about was herself. Herself and her precious drink.

She knew what her mother would be doing right now. She could see her stretching for the bottle of gin as if she were in the room with her.

'Tea's ready in half an hour,' said her Mum.

That surprised Debbie. Usually, she had to get her own tea. She gave her school bag a kick and wondered, just for a moment, whether she should run into the kitchen. Say she was sorry. Talk to her about the drinking. But what was the point?

'See if I care!' she yelled, before stamping angrily up the stairs.

We learn the same information in this second passage but entirely from Debbie's point-of-view. Single-person viewpoint makes the passage more powerful and emotionally involving: less confusing. There is no mistaking which character the reader is supposed to identify with.

Multiple viewpoint is best reserved for straight adventure stories, where all the attention is focused on the action and we never really need to know what the characters are feeling and thinking. You can also use multiple viewpoint as a deliberate ploy, but you do need to structure your story in such a way that it doesn't become confusing. For example, if I had wanted to write from both Debbie's point-of-view and Mum's point-of-view I should have dealt with the two characters individually, making a distinct break whenever I changed viewpoint.

In *Flour Babies,* Anne Fine begins the book from the teacher, Mr Cartright's, viewpoint. She then makes a break at the end of Chapter One and switches to the viewpoint of the main character, Simon Martin. If it is absolutely necessary to have more than one viewpoint, this is a much better way of handling the change.

In *Stone Cold,* Robert Swindells uses first person multiple viewpoint; the book is written from the viewpoint of two different people, a homeless teenager and a serial killer. He alternates between the two and the switch is underlined by using two different typefaces for the two different characters. However, I should stress that it does take a great deal of skill to pull off a book written in this way. After all, you have two characters to know inside-out rather than one! For the inexperienced children's writer, it is simpler, wherever possible, to stick to the third person singular viewpoint.

Viewpoint: Exercise

- Write a conversation between two people, writing it first from both viewpoints; then from one viewpoint using third person singular; then from one viewpoint using first person. Which one comes most naturally to you? Which works the best?

CHAPTER FOURTEEN

STYLE

Beatrix Potter, Rudyard Kipling, A. A. Milne, Lewis Carroll – all the great children's writers have their own individual, very recognisable, style.

Who could mistake ...

> Once upon a time there were four little Rabbits, and their names were – Flopsy, Mopsy, Cotton-tail and Peter. They lived with their Mother in a sand-bank, underneath the root of a very big fir-tree.

... as anything other than Beatrix Potter?

Or ...

> Here is Edward Bear, coming downstairs now, bump, bump, bump on the back of his head, behind Christopher Robin.

... as anything other than A. A. Milne?

Many modern authors, too, have become known for their unique style – authors such as Roald Dahl, Philip Ridley, Paul Jennings, Dick King-Smith.

The temptation, for the new children's writer, is to copy the style of such authors rather than develop a style of their own. Sometimes this is done deliberately – particularly when the established author is dead: a new author admires an established author's books and decides to be the 'next' whoever it is.

But sometimes it is done subconsciously. After all, it makes sense that you are only going to want to write in a style that you, yourself, enjoy reading.

Either way, imitation of another author's writing style rarely works. You will be rumbled. Occasionally, it may be possible to use elements of a recognisable style to help you develop a style of your own but, for the most part, style is something that it is almost impossible to imitate successfully.

Establishing a strong style is all-important. Very often an editor will admit that there is nothing particularly *wrong* with a submitted story but, when pushed to give a reason for rejecting it, will say, rather vaguely, 'It just wasn't *strong* enough' or 'It just wasn't *special* enough'. What they actually mean by this is that the writing didn't have a sufficiently individual style to make it stand out from all the other, equally satisfactorily mediocre, stories in the slush pile.

So how do you establish a unique style that is going to make an editor sit up and take notice?

BALANCE

The first thing that will discourage an editor – because it will consequently discourage a child – is pages and pages of uninterrupted narrative. Great blocks of text are boring to look at and a struggle to read.

So keep your paragraphs short, whatever age you are writing for, and make sure that you have a good balance of dialogue and narrative. Remember that dialogue when it goes on for too long can also become very confusing, as the reader tries to remember who is speaking. If you concentrate on establishing this ideal balance, you will be forced to use dialogue only to move the plot forwards (or, occasionally, to reveal character).

The following was an opening to a short story sent to my editorial advice service by a new writer:

I was suddenly wide awake, but I could not work out why. I knew that, in my sleep, I had heard something but I didn't know what. I lay very still. There was nothing, not a sound. I waited a minute or two and then relaxed enough to turn over. At that moment it happened again, not loud, just a sort of drumming noise. It seemed to be coming from above my room, but there was nothing up there except the loft.

This is a very long, laboured first paragraph. The story went on:

It was the first night ever that I had been left alone in the house. Although I was thirteen several months ago, my parents did not want to leave me. Usually if they go out in the evening, my sister Sophie is here too. She's only ten and so I don't mind them fixing a baby-sitter. This time she had gone away with them to see our Gran who was ill, and I was allowed to stay here because of the big game the next day.

Dear me! I've almost forgotten why I'm reading this story. And still no sign of any dialogue ...

I waited; it happened again. The only things in the loft are a few old cases and cardboard boxes of Christmas decorations, things like that. And, of course, the railway. My grandfather is mad about model trains. When Granny died – that's the other one, not the one who is ill at the moment – he moved into a special flat and so his railway moved here. I really enjoy running the trains too. But they don't run on their own in the middle of the night ...

In fact, this is a potentially exciting and very tense situation, but any drama that might be there is completely submerged by the lengthy narrative. No editor would read beyond the first couple of pages. However, the author was determined that his story be accepted for publication and so we agreed to help him knock it into shape.

The first person viewpoint had to be dropped. This is an action-led story for 8–12-year-olds and third person singular viewpoint is far more suitable for this type of story.

We suggested using shorter snappier sentences to grab the attention and add punch, but also to increase the feeling of tension. As it stands, no emotion is being portrayed at all. Surely the boy would have been frightened?

A younger, more colloquial 'voice' was needed to tell the story. The opening above is grammatically correct, but it doesn't read like the voice of a 14-year-old boy.

The narrative needed to be broken up with dialogue, to move the story and add pace and momentum.

The author took our suggestions to heart, and a few days later we received version number two:

Nick sat bolt upright in bed. He'd heard a noise. He was sure of it. He reached under the bed for his baseball bat, then crept across his room to the open door.

'Who's that?' he shouted.

His voice echoed round the dark, empty house. But then he heard it again. That was it, a sort of rumbling, drumming noise. Where was it coming from, inside or outside? There it was again, up above, in the attic.

Nick took a deep, shaky breath. It was the first night that he'd been left alone in the house. Mum and Dad had gone to see Gran because she'd just been rushed into hospital and, of course, Sophie had gone too. There'd been quite a row because Mum had said he couldn't stay on his own, but it was the big game tomorrow, and he was captain.

'I'm fourteen, for heaven's sake,' he'd argued.

'Yes, let him stay,' Dad had agreed. 'There's got to be a first time. I'll make sure Bob's home this weekend.'

'Well, I'm still not happy,' said Mum, 'but if you promise to ring Uncle Bob if there's any problem, I suppose . . .'

Now Nick stood shaking in his bedroom doorway. He heard the noise again, right above his head.

'There's nothing in the attic except a few old cases and cardboard boxes, Christmas decorations, things like that,' he thought. 'And Grandpa's railway.'

The story, *Ghost Train* by John West, was accepted for publication by Orion Children's Books and included in an anthology of short stories in their Quids for Kids series. And you can see why.

Show Don't Tell

In the first version of that story, there was too much long-winded 'telling' and not enough 'showing'.

'I was suddenly wide awake.' How can we visualise that? What happens when a person wakes from a deep sleep? Some people emerge slowly, floating between consciousness and unconsciousness for several minutes; others open their eyes suddenly and freeze. Others sit bolt upright, or leap out of bed. Whatever it is you think your character would do in this situation, it is far better, stylistically, to *describe* it to the reader, so they can get a detailed picture in their mind's eye of what happens. If someone is angry, *show* that they are angry. Perhaps their jaw is visibly clenched, or their fists. Perhaps their face has gone red, or white.

If someone is frightened, *show* it. We can clearly see, in the second version of the story, that Nick is frightened. He grabs his baseball bat. He takes a shaky breath. He stands shaking in his bedroom doorway. It is these little details that will add colour and depth to your writing and give your stories life.

A Style That Fits

Your writing style should suit the type of story that you're writing. If you are writing a contemporary 'real-life' story, then your writing style must have more punch and pace than if you are writing a historical drama, in which you need to capture the spirit of a bygone age.

Jill Paton Walsh uses a particularly distinctive writing style in *A Parcel of Patterns*, which tells the story of the plague, brought to the village of Eyam in a parcel of patterns from London:

> So I took my leave of her, and went home quiet and full of thought, and set about putting a rabbit to cook upon the spit, and to chopping the last few boughs of sage. Someone might yet have need of it. And now that Goody Trickett was lost, people came hoping to me, that I might know a little of what she knew. All my wisdom was sage tea; of that I made pansful.

Even if characters *didn't* speak like that back then – and we have no means of knowing – the idiom gives a distinct impression of another, very different, time.

DON'T BE AFRAID OF SAID

I am always amazed at the endless alternatives new writers come up with to replace the word 'said'.

'Why not use "said"?' she argued/gasped/demanded/muttered/cried.

Sometimes I think writers are trying to prove that they have such a large vocabulary that they never need to use any verb more than once.

The fact is that the reader doesn't notice how many times an author uses 'he said' 'she said'. But the reader *will* notice – and remark upon its strangeness and artificiality – every time an alternative is used. 'Said' is hardly registered, except to tell the reader who is doing the speaking. That is the only reason it is there, after all. It is *what* is being said that the reader should be encouraged to focus on.

TITLES AND FIRST LINES

Titles and opening lines are more important than many of us like to believe. I'm not suggesting, for one minute, that it's something you should spend hours fretting over before you've written a single word. Indeed, the opposite may be true: finish your book first and *then* return to the opening pages. Often a title will only occur to you when you have written the book. When the book is finished, and your perspective is more objective, it is quite common to feel that the story would work better starting in a different place, or in a different way.

A writer once came to me at my Advice Centre, asking me to look at a book she had written for 8–12-year-olds. Simultaneously, she had also submitted the manuscript to a large publishing house where I happened to be doing some freelance work.

'What's Ruth's manuscript like?' I asked the editor she'd sent it to – I hadn't yet had a chance to look at it myself.

'I've had a quick glance at it,' the editor replied. 'Doesn't grab me.'

A few days later, I cleared a space on my desk and started to read Ruth's manuscript. Because of what the editor said I wasn't hopeful.

As I began to read, my worst fears were confirmed. The title of the story was *Summertime Santas*, which conjured up a Christmas story with a bit of summer-holiday adventure thrown in. Every editor's nightmare – a book with a seasonal theme and, therefore, a very limited sale. And the first chapter was toe-curdlingly amateurish.

However, I was being paid to assess this story and give editorial advice and assess it I would. Which meant reading the whole thing, no matter how awful it was.

But by the end of Chapter Two, I was hooked. I read the rest at one sitting. The first thing I did was pick up the phone and tell Ruth how wonderful I thought her story was and that I would do anything to see it published. But she'd have to lose the first chapter – and the title.

Eighteen months later that book was published by Puffin – the same publisher who had, originally, been doubtful. *The Master of Secrets* by Ruth Symes was a great success.

The reason I am telling you this story is obvious. If I hadn't been paid to read the whole of that book I, as an editor, would never have got past the title and the first chapter. It would have joined the pile of rejections and the author would probably never have known the reason why.

I suppose you could say that this story is a lesson for publishers rather than authors. Ideally, we should never give up on a book until we've read the whole thing. But this isn't an ideal world. Sadly, editors don't have the time or resources to read more than the beginning – if that doesn't grab them, they'll abandon it. So try to ensure that your beginning 'hooks' the reader from the very first sentence. Establish tension, intrigue – make them want to read on, to find out what is going to happen. The title is equally important in the long run, as it will be used to sell the book to the customer; however, publishers will be prepared to come up with a title for you if they think your work has potential. But why not prove your talent by creating your own?

THE LAST WORD

New authors often worry about language. How complicated should the language they use be?

Stop worrying. This is only an issue when writing for the educational market. The language you use should be as simple as possible. You shouldn't simplify things to such an extent that you are patronising the child reader; but, on the other hand, you should be aware of words and sentence structures that children may not understand.

One of my students wrote a Picture Book based on the expression 'I've got the hump'. She insisted that it was an expression young children would understand. I had my doubts and asked my own children if they understood the expression. They didn't, but, I reasoned, they could be the exception rather than the rule. It wasn't until I was discussing the subject with another editor that the real problem became clear to me.

'It doesn't really matter whether some children understand the expression or not,' she pointed out. 'If there is *any doubt at all*, then don't use it.'

When writing for children, you are aiming at clarity of expression. You are not trying to impress them with your intellectual achievements. If you write with the mind of a child (and the skill of an adult), you can't go far wrong.

Style: Exercises
- Think of some titles for any story ideas you may have. Would they make you want to read the book they are selling?
- Choose one of your ideas and write an eye-catching opening paragraph, making sure that it is your own unique voice you are using.

III

BEING
PUBLISHED

CHAPTER FIFTEEN

PRESENTATION AND APPROACH

'If the washing machine is turned off by a power failure, it will restart automatically from the position is stopped at, adjusting accordingly.'

This may not read like a passage from a bestselling novel but when John Howard, an aspiring children's writer, rewrote the instructions to his washing machine and called it *The Tin Drum,* many of the literary agents and publishers he sent it to wrote back rejection letters saying how much they had enjoyed it.

Ridiculous – maybe. But all I can say is that John Howard has obviously never had to deal with a publisher's slush pile on a day-to-day basis. Believe me, some days, even a rewritten washing-machine manual has more potential than some of the drivel that wings its way into the reader's in tray.

The number of unsolicited manuscripts a publisher receives will depend on its profile and size. The smaller, lesser-known publishers receive maybe a few submissions a day, whereas large publishers may well receive hundreds a week. The one thing that *is* certain is that *all* publishers receive more unsolicited manuscripts than they would ideally like.

But it needn't be this way. The only reason editors groan when faced with the slush pile is that so few unsolicited submissions reach even a minimum standard. Few writers research the market before approaching publishers (you already have a head start because you have read this book) – and that's not the worst omission by any means.

Sometimes the covering letter is so badly written that the editor knows the writer has no hope of being able to a construct a full-length story. Sometimes the manuscript is illegible – either because of bad handwriting or worn-out typewriter ribbon. Sometimes it's impossible to even open the envelope!

John Howard came up with his *Tin Drum* idea to prove a point – that publishers don't read unsolicited manuscripts. In my opinion the fact that he received polite rejection letters back proves nothing. Rejection letters are standard and their language is designed to let the writer down lightly. Faced with a rewritten washing-machine manual, they are hardly likely to waste time writing a personal rejection letter pointing out exactly where the author went wrong!

The main thing to remember when submitting a manuscript is not to give the publisher any excuse to reject your work without proper consideration. Publishers *want* to find good new writers, and readers and editors live in terror of missing the next blockbuster. All publishers have tales of rejecting books that went on to be bestsellers with another publishing house. If your work looks professional, your covering letter is intriguing and your submission fits the list of the publisher to whom you have sent it, you can be almost certain that it will not be cast aside completely unread. Presentation and approach are what it is all about.

RESEARCH THE MARKET

Researching the market you are writing for isn't just a case of relying on the few books that you have at home for your own children/grandchildren/pupils. Research requires some effort and I would expect a writer to have spent weeks, if not months, doing this research before even so much as *touching* a keyboard.

Buy, or borrow, as many titles as you can. Read them. Analyse them. Read them again . . . and again . . . and again! There is no substitute for reading as much current children's fiction as possible.

If you have been following this book section by section, you will already have a good idea as to how to go about doing a certain amount of research through children's libraries and bookshops (and by completing the exercises listed at the end of each chapter). There is also a wide range of organisations and publications available designed to help people who want to become involved in the children's book world – more about these in the last chapter of this book.

Something else that you should be doing is collecting children's publisher's catalogues and editorial guidelines (if available). This is by far the best way of keeping in touch with the types of books that the different publishers are producing and will give you a good feel for the market. Catalogues are available, by request, from publisher's marketing departments and most publishers these days put their catalogues online as well. Editorial guidelines are available from the relevant editorial department – but note that guidelines are only likely to be available if that publisher accepts unsolicited manuscripts. A simple phone call should be enough to elicit these precious publications, although sometimes publishers prefer the request to be made in writing or by email.

Once you have the information in front of you, you need to analyse it carefully. Note the different profiles that publishers have. Some, such as Scholastic Children's Books, specialise in mass-market paperback fiction; Lion Children's Books takes Christian values into the general marketplace.

How to Choose a Publisher

As I've already said, choosing a publisher comes down to thoroughly researching the market. By carefully studying guides such as *The Children's Writers' & Artists' Yearbook* you can find out who is publishing the type of books that you want to write.

However, increasingly, publishers are making the decision not to accept unsolicited manuscripts. This is particularly true of the larger publishing houses and another good reason to concentrate on smaller publishing houses instead. Publishing houses that have made this decision will only look at work that comes via a reputable literary agent known to one of their editors. So it makes sense to spend some time approaching literary agents as well as publishers. The best agents are unlikely to take you seriously until you have had something published and have a proven track record. But there's no harm in giving this approach a go.

When approaching agents it is even more important to spell out that you are serious about a writing career and don't only have the one book up your sleeve. With agents it is best to send a few samples of your writing if you can.

However, it is not, as many writers believe, a 'chicken-and-egg' situation – particularly not with publishers. There are many publishers out there still looking at unsolicited manuscripts and there are some agents who will take a risk on an unpublished author. It is worth noting that every single success we have ever had at The Writers' Advice Centre became published without first having an agent. Becoming a successful children's author is more about self-belief, hard work and determination, rather than raw talent. Having a cracking good story to tell also helps!

Phone Calls, Enquiry Letters and Appointments

A common concern of any new writer is whether or not they should phone, or write to, a publisher *before* they submit any work. My general advice would be, don't. *All* publishers are keen to find good new writers – it is, after all, where their future profits lie. Even publishers who claim they do not consider unsolicited material, or who state that their lists are full, will make room for a new piece of work if they think it has commercial potential.

If you *do* make a phone call, remember that publishers' offices are busy places and staff do not want to chat at length with total strangers. Get to the point quickly. Do not complain that the reader/editor is hard to get hold of (even if they are) and do not start by telling them how wonderful your story is (even if it is).

Take the opportunity to check the name of the editor to whom you should make the submission (and check the spelling of the name and address). If asked how long your story is, do not say 'quite long', or 'quite short', or 'oh, about 72 pages'. After all, it could be handwritten, typed, single-spaced, double-spaced, have two words per page etc. Give the number of words – and count them *before* you make the call.

If asked what your story is about, do not say: 'I would rather not give too much away/It is in the hands of my solicitor/The idea is patented'. Just give them an idea of the theme and style – as briefly as possible.

Enquiry letters are a complete waste of time unless you are requesting a catalogue or editorial guidelines. Letters that state, 'I have written a children's story. Would you be interested in looking at it?' are particularly pointless and will probably end up in the bin. After all, you should have enough confidence in your own work – and have researched the market sufficiently – to *know* that the publisher will be interested in looking at it.

No reader or editor will give you an appointment to see them unless they have first seen your work – they don't have the time. And don't turn up unannounced at their office and expect anything other than polite excuses – you will not get past the front desk.

If you are going to try an individual style of approach, do be careful. Sometimes these are intriguing; sometimes they are amateur at best.

For example, I once received a series of 'teasers', each one addressed specifically to me. They were colourful, professional computer print-outs, showing a football pitch with strap lines 'in the football vernacular' in large print:

> I was sick as a parrot – unnamed source who missed out on Gillbert.
>   The boy done good – the man who signed Gillbert.
>   Some of the crowd are on the pitch – advance order mayhem for Gillbert,
>   Gillbert ready for kick-off.

And, finally:

> 'Ere we go, 'ere we go, 'ere we go – Gillbert arrives on Monday.

And arrive it did, to earn my immediate attention. Sadly, it wasn't quite right and was returned with a personal rejection letter:

Gillbert put on transfer market. Failed to live up to early potential – unnamed talent-spotter who picked up on Gillbert.

Another author tried similar but less appealing tactics, which, as far as I was concerned, badly backfired.

I received, first, a rather poorly made badge stating: *One Sandwich Short of a Picnic*; and second, an empty sandwich packet in a Jiffy bag. I found this approach at best, tasteless and, at worst, threatening. When I eventually received the manuscript, I'm afraid I sent it straight back. I subsequently received a very unpleasant letter from the author complaining that I hadn't commented on his original approach.

If you don't feel you can pull off a PR stunt successfully, then stick to more conventional tactics!

THE COVERING LETTER

'I have wrote this book . . .'

Atrocious English. But you would be amazed how many letters publishers receive from aspiring children's authors that start in exactly this way. Would it make you believe the author can write?

So the first thing to get right when approaching publishers with your work is the covering letter.

You *must* send one – it should be individually adapted to the requirements of each publisher you approach. It should be short (one A4 page), to the point and, preferably, typed. Remember to send it to a name (not Sir/Madam), to date it and sign it.

Bear in mind that publishers do *not* want to know who else has read your manuscript and enjoyed it – your granny, your neighbour's little girl etc., and it is not a good idea to send copies of rejection letters from other publishers. Why let them know that other people don't want your work – unless it has had a very near miss and was ultimately rejected for reasons that won't make it less appealing elsewhere.

The other thing that publishers don't want to read in a covering letter is your life history. Some writers seem to find it necessary to impart the minutest details about why they wrote the book in the first place, their personal circumstances, their state of health . . . On the other hand, there is a happy medium to be struck – one letter I received the other day simply said, 'A 10,000-word Christmas story. Any chance?'

Other 'don'ts' in the covering letter: *don't* say that you have written 'a series of children's books' (unless it's been published!) or state that your idea has enormous potential for merchandising – and that you have already designed the T-shirt and stuffed the cuddly toy. No publisher will take on a series until the first book has been a proven success. And to come up with an idea for merchandising before acceptance is jumping the gun by a very long way.

A covering letter should say: what your story is about (one line); how long it is (number of words); and how you think it will fit into the publisher's programme. It should also mention in passing any previously published work or other relevant experience.

Here is an example of a covering letter that, if all else fails, I suggest you use as a template:

[Date]

[Address]

Dear [Editor's full name]

I enclose my manuscript *The Wizard's Skip*.

This is a humorous, fantasy adventure story for five- to eight-year-olds and is about a boy who finds a video game in a skip. It is 3000 words in length and I see it fitting into your *Banana Book* series.

I am a teacher by training and have three children of my own, all under ten. I have had a few articles published in local publications and edit our church newsletter. This is my first children's book.

I look forward to hearing your reactions to *The Wizard's Skip*.

Yours sincerely,

[Name]

On the other hand, you could go for the more witty approach. The following paragraph is from a covering letter I received. It amused me enormously:

So please read and reject – for every rejection letter I've promised myself an entire M&S Victoria Sponge with Earl Grey on-the-side to commiserate with – so I would greatly appreciate hearing from you. And in case you're thinking I'm gonna put on a lot of weight because the enclosed is just awful – plan (b) is to become the fattest (unpublished) writer in Tunbridge Wells! See – faultless planning!

MANUSCRIPT PRESENTATION

Your manuscript should be typed (preferably double-spaced), as error-free and clean as possible, using one side of A4 white paper only. It doesn't have to be prepared on a state-of-the-art Apple Mac but, if you are going to write seriously, you will probably want to invest in some kind of computer or laptop. Machines can be bought inexpensively these days and once you have one you will wonder how you ever managed without.

Your manuscript should not be bound, stapled or paperclipped – particularly annoying is when authors paper-clip or staple each individual chapter, making them unmanageable to read. I suggest putting the manuscript loose in a strong cardboard folder. Label the front of the folder with the title of the manuscript and your name and address. Put your name and address on the title page, together with the number of words. Number the pages and put your name and address on the last page of the manuscript.

If you are submitting a longer novel – anything over 15,000 words – I suggest enclosing the first three or four chapters and a *brief* synopsis. By a synopsis, I do mean just that – not a chapter-by-chapter outline. All editors really want to know, if they like the first few chapters, is the direction the story is going to take. If they want to know what happens chapter by chapter, they will ask for the rest of the manuscript.

If your story is under 15,000 words, I would suggest sending the whole thing, perhaps with a synopsis for good measure.

If it is a Picture Book, it is a good idea to enclose a dummy, a separate copy of the text divided into pages and a copy of the text 'straight' (i.e. undivided).

Presenting non-fiction is slightly different. Some things to include in your book proposal are:

- Information about yourself, including any expertise that makes you particularly well qualified to write this book.
- If you have been previously published, include a list of credits if they are relevant.
- If there are other books similar to yours on the market, list them and show how yours offers something different.
- Describe your book briefly, including details of chapters, highlights, organisation etc. Use your table of contents as the skeleton for this. If you are a new writer, or new to this publisher, enclose a couple of sample chapters, or the entire MS if it is short (as with a Picture Book).
- Describe briefly how you see your proposal fitting into the publisher's current list. (Obtain, first, catalogues for any publisher you target from their customer service operation).
- If you are targeting a particular readership, tell your publisher and provide reasons why this is a particularly good market. If you envisage a series of books, mention the possibility but do not go into detail.
- If you have a particular way of marketing your book – for example, if you are a teacher and can use it for INSET training – you could include this.

COPYRIGHT

Don't worry about copyrighting your work. Some authors go to the most extraordinary lengths to protect their submissions but, contrary to popular belief, publishers are not in the habit of stealing ideas.

In Britain, you hold the copyright for your work as soon as it is written down – you do not need to apply for copyright or register your work with any organisation. The only exception to this is when you are writing as part of your employment – for instance, if you are a journalist working for a newspaper. Copyright lasts for 70 years after the end of the calendar year in which an author dies.

There is no copyright over ideas – so always get an idea down in writing. Similarly, there is no copyright over titles, although you could be accused of 'passing off' if you used a well-known title for your own work.

If you are still concerned about proving that you are the copyright holder of an unpublished work, you can post a copy of your manuscript to yourself and keep this, unopened. The postmark will provide proof that you wrote the work by a certain date. Or you can deposit a copy of your manuscript with a bank or solicitor (get a dated receipt). If you are worried about protecting your idea from being copied when you send your work to agents or publishers, *The Writer's Handbook* suggests that you ask anyone who sees your work to sign a letter confirming that they will not use those ideas or disclose them to anyone else, although, in practise, it can be difficult to get them to sign such a letter. Remember, too, that publishers and agents receive so much unsolicited material that they may already be considering work that is similar to your own.

The Society of Authors publishes a series of leaflets on various aspects of copyright law, priced at £2 each. Contact: The Society of Authors, 84 Drayton Gardens, London, SW10 9SB (tel: 020 7373 6642).

REJECTION

Be prepared for it!

Enclose return postage. Publishers simply cannot be expected to fund return postage of manuscripts for the hundreds of unsolicited submissions they receive.

Either enclose an envelope or packaging ready stamped and addressed, or send stamps together with, preferably, a sticky self-addressed label. Personally, I prefer the latter – it removes the temptation for an editor to pop your manuscript straight into the return envelope without even looking at it!

It is reasonable to expect a publisher to take anything up to three months to consider your work, so it is perfectly acceptable to submit your work to two or three publishers at any one time – my own personal opinion is that it is much better not to tell each one that you have done this. However, some editors believe it is better to state that your offering is a multiple submission as, if a publisher is keen, they will be forced to move more quickly than they might have done otherwise. The opposing argument is that it is possible the publisher will take your work less seriously than if you had offered it to them exclusively.

Authors tend to worry that if they do approach more than one publisher at once, they will receive multiple offers and upset people all round. All I can say to that is, you should be so lucky!

What I would recommend against is sending out your work to every publisher you've ever heard of. If you do this, and they all reject your manuscript, you have left yourself with nowhere to go should you decide that it is possible to revise your work in order to make it more marketable. Publishers are very reluctant to view a piece of work twice even if it has been revised. And, believe me, they have long memories!

Rejection letters are usually fairly standard. A publisher seldom has the time to give you a specific reason for rejection so letters will often include polite and largely meaningless phrases such as 'we enjoyed your work but I'm afraid it isn't quite right for us'. If you do get a personally worded rejection letter (and do remember that a letter can often *look* personal but be 'mass-produced') take it in the spirit in which it is intended. It is all too easy to react with anger to criticism, but an editor wouldn't take the trouble to give that criticism if they didn't feel that your writing showed promise. If you really can't stomach the advice then put the letter away for a few days/weeks/months until you feel you can go and look at it with some objectivity. *Don't*, whatever you do, let the editor know that you are angry. You would be amazed at how many abusive letters editors receive from rejected authors. Making an enemy of an editor can only harm you in the long run, and, in any case, it is unreasonable to be unpleasant to someone simply for doing their job.

Often, criticism will be backed up with a phrase such as 'we would be happy to see more of your work'. Again, take this in the spirit in which it is meant. Don't just post off another story that you happen to have on file but work on something new, specifically targeted at that publisher, and send it in as soon as you can. When you do so, remind the editor of who you are and what it was you sent in last time. They won't necessarily remember, but they will know that if they said they wanted to see more of your work they liked your original submission.

There are many reasons for rejection. It could be because your writing isn't good enough – but it could be because the publishers already have a similar story on their list. Alternatively, it could be down to personal taste. All editors try to be objective, but they are bound to look more favourably on material that they themselves enjoy.

Sometimes an editor will tell you that your work wasn't 'strong' enough. An agent friend of mine believes that, when an editor says that, it's a sure sign that they haven't read the manuscript. I disagree. When most editors say something isn't strong enough, they mean just that there's nothing wrong with it, but it has nothing sufficiently special to make it stand out from the competition.

Try to turn rejection into a positive learning experience. One writer I know received a simply-worded rejection letter from an editor saying that she liked the story but 'it wasn't quite right'. She would have thought no more of it had the editor not mistakenly also enclosed her report on the story for the editorial meeting. It was extremely damning!

However, once she'd recovered from the shock (and it took her several days, if not weeks), she read and re-read that report, taking every single comment on board. Her feeling was that this unfortunate oversight had occurred for a reason – and that reason was to make her a better writer.

She has now published six books, with six more in the pipeline.

CHAPTER SIXTEEN

ACCEPTANCE

Acceptance of your book for publication is every author's dream. It is what you have been striving for. It is the reason you wrote it. It is the reason you have worked so hard completing all the exercises in this book! It doesn't matter how much you tell yourself that you enjoy writing for its own sake – the fact is, we all want formal recognition for what we do, and an offer of publication provides that recognition.

Every writer who has submitted a manuscript to a publisher waits with baited breath for some kind of response. The post is eyed warily every day. Is that big, bulky package your returned manuscript? If no bulky package arrives, then does that nice, clean, white envelope contain the offer of your dreams?

Forget it. It's more than likely that the process of acceptance will take a much more complicated and lengthy route.

Often, it will be a question of building up a relationship with an editor over a long period of time. It may start with a personal rejection letter saying that, although this particular manuscript isn't quite right, they would be happy to see more of your work. More work duly wings its way in the right direction and, after perhaps another rejection or two, the editor may invite you in for 'a chat'.

All publishers (and agents) need to assess the marketability of their authors. They need to know that you don't have only one book in you, that if they publish your book, you will be able to provide more work of the same standard. They want to be reassured that you are committed as a writer, that you are versatile and that, as a personality, you are someone they can work with. They want to know whether – and how – they can promote you as an author. They are, in short, looking on you as an investment – because that's exactly what you are. Few first books make money, so the publisher needs to be sure that, even if they lose money on your first book, they are going to have more than one bite at the apple.

For this reason, publishers don't like their authors spreading themselves too thinly. They like authors to be loyal to them, and them alone. So if you get as far as the 'chatting' stage – even if you know that you are planning to work with other publishing houses – be as positive and as upbeat as possible. It's a bit like a job interview – ultimately you don't *have* to take the job, but you need to give the impression that you want it more than any other.

Even after the interview is over, you will probably still not have a promise of a formal offer. The editor may ask you to do some more work on your manuscript – or may suggest that you try writing a completely different book for a specific slot. If I were you, I would go along with the editor for as long as you feel is reasonable. After all, as an unpublished writer, you have nothing to lose.

The only time to start talking money is if they ask to take your book to one of the book fairs. At that stage it may be reasonable to ask for some kind of development fee and, to be fair, most reputable publishers will offer this without you having to ask.

However, as far as revising manuscripts is concerned, I'm afraid that is just part and parcel of being a new writer. A publisher is under no obligation to accept your work, even after *hundreds* of rewrites, if they still don't like it. Most publishers, in any case, don't have the time to encourage authors unless they genuinely feel that both sides are going to benefit at the end of it all.

OFFER

The day comes. The offer letter finally arrives. All your hard work has been worthwhile and you are about to become a published children's author at last.

Wrong!

I don't want to be negative, but I have seen too many disappointed authors not to offer a few words of warning at this stage. *Nothing* is certain in publishing until you have the published book in your hands. I have seen contracts signed, advances paid – and *still* the book has been cancelled.

I had a phone call from one author the other day who had been excitedly waiting for the publication day of her first Picture Book. She'd been paid the advance, she'd approved the cover and the illustrations, she'd seen her name appear in the catalogue – she'd done everything, except see the finished copy. And then, four weeks before publication date, the foreign publisher, with whom a co-edition had been lined up, cancelled the contract, and the whole deal collapsed. To say she was disappointed would be an understatement!

It probably won't happen to you, but it *might*. Forewarned is forearmed.

The offer letter will generally get straight to the point. It will say that the publisher likes your book and is happy to make an offer to publish it. It will offer an advance, set against royalties, usually payable in two (or sometimes three) stages – half on signature of the contract and half on publication, or one third on signature, one third on acceptance of the typescript in a state ready for publication, and one third on actual publication. An advance is literally that – the publisher is advancing you potential earnings. You will not receive royalties (i.e. a percentage of the sale price of each book sold) until the advance has 'earned out' – in other words, until your book has earned more money for the publisher than your advance was worth.

The letter will also talk about rights. Usually, nowadays, the offer is likely to cover both hardback and paperback rights (although most children's books go straight into paperback), but the publisher will also want to 'control' other rights, meaning that they can sell the book to other markets – in America, in translation, to large print publishers, to magazines ... Agents tend to hang on to these rights on behalf of their authors and then do the selling themselves but if you don't have an agent, a publisher will expect what is called 'world rights'. You will be given a percentage of every additional rights sale made by your publisher or agent.

The letter will probably mention a provisional timescale – when they would like delivery of the completed text, and when they plan to publish the book.

The next move is down to you. You can either accept straight away (and if it's your first book you'll be very tempted!), or you can give the offer a little thought (and then accept it), or you can negotiate on any points that concern you. But remember that despite every inexperienced author's belief that all publishers are out to 'do' the writer, most publishers have very standard terms and conditions for books that they take on to their list.

The first thing you will realise is that you won't get rich quick by writing for children. Advances vary depending on the type and length of the book and this is set against royalties, which are, again, fairly standard. A royalty isn't always on offer. For short stories, a flat fee is usually paid (which can often seem derisory) and the author will rarely see any additional income.

You are perfectly entitled to try to 'up' the advance if you feel it is too low. However, as most publishers offer standard amounts and don't expect to make much of a profit on a new writer in any case, there is usually little room for negotiation. The bottom line, with a first book, is that the publisher holds all the cards. And they can always cancel if they feel you are being difficult. If you have good reason to believe that the terms you are being offered are genuinely unreasonable then do take it up with them – as politely as possible! The Society of Authors will advise you on this – more about them later.

The one area of the offer letter that you can negotiate on is the timescale factor. More often than not with a first book, you will already have written the complete text and it will be a case of revision only. However, even revision can take time, so do make sure that you can deliver on the date that they say. It is much better to ask for more time at this early stage than to let publishers down at the last minute, when your book has already been scheduled.

THE CONTRACT

Once you have negotiated the basic terms, you will, at some stage, be sent a formal contract to sign, after which you usually receive half of the advance payable. I say 'at some stage' because it can seem like for ever before the contract actually arrives, and even longer before you receive any money. Often, you will be well along the road to publication before you see any sign of a contract.

The whole subject of contracts is too vast and complicated to be covered in a book like this, so I will just mention a few points to look out for:

Do read your contract from start to finish, even if you think it looks too complicated for you to understand. Even though, as mentioned above, most publishers have standard contracts, don't feel that you can't query clauses, or make changes to the contract (within reason).

Obviously, you need to check that the delivery date is the same as the one you discussed after receiving your offer letter, and think again whether it is reasonable for you.

If your work has been commissioned but not yet accepted in its completed form, be very careful over any wording alluding to the publisher having no obligation to accept the finished work if deemed unacceptable. It is right and proper that a publisher should have an escape clause if they have misjudged the capabilities of the author – but to be fair to the author, they must be able to justify their rejection and give the author the opportunity to bring their work up to standard.

Don't agree to the publisher being able to edit your work without your approval. When Malorie Blackman's Picture Book *That New Dress* was published in the States, the American publisher wanted to change the last three words of the book from 'And Mum smiled' to 'And Mum sighed'. This was a tiny change but, in fact, changed the whole ending of the book from satisfactory to rather unsatisfactory. It's a point worth bearing in mind – remember just how crucial even small changes can be.

Watch out for any clauses giving the publisher the right to publish the author's next work. Contracts usually do contain this clause and, while publishers may not agree to remove it, at least get them to ensure that the clause doesn't act to the detriment of you, the author. One author I know agreed to just such a clause and then, after publication of his first book (which was very successful), found that the publisher wouldn't either agree or disagree to publish another book. They stalled on everything that he offered them but, because of the terms of his contract, he couldn't threaten to take his work elsewhere.

Rights is another section of the contract that authors get hot under the collar about, particularly in this electronic age when audio, radio, television, film, video, animation and electronic multimedia rights are all assuming greater importance than they used to. In fact, some contracts still don't make specific provision for some of these rights. Remember that the selling of various rights is just another way in which you and your publisher can make money from your book. If you don't have an agent to sell the rights for you, then the publisher will undertake to do it. They will want to sell the rights – and generate extra income – as much as you do! It is just worth checking whether they can sell rights without consulting you first to get your agreement on any rights deal.

If you are concerned about your contract and don't have anyone to advise you, my suggestion would be that you join The Society of Authors (see Page 154). It is relatively cheap to become a provisional member and their legal team will vet the contract for you. This means that you are getting legal advice for a reasonable fee from someone who knows a great deal about publishing contracts – which are quite different from any contract you've ever seen before. They also publish a very good *Quick Guide to Publishing Contracts,* which is inexpensive and written by experts.

WORKING TOWARDS PUBLICATION

To start with, you will be assigned an editor who will work with you on revisions and changes. It is important to build up a good relationship with your editor and to trust his or her judgement. If you don't agree with any changes, then say so, but try not to quibble unless you feel particularly strongly about a change. If your objections are reasonable, it is more than likely that your editor will agree with you – or have a very good reason not to. However, there is absolutely no point in establishing a reputation for being what every editor dreads: a 'difficult author'. In that case, your publisher will only be less likely to want to work with you again.

If your book is a Picture Book or heavily illustrated Reader, you may be consulted on the choice of illustrator. But as a general rule the publisher is the best judge of which illustrative style best suits your text. Even if you had your heart set on one particular illustrator, the chances are that they may not necessarily have the time to fit in with the publishing schedule. Often, it is a question of trying two or three illustrators before one finally works out in every respect.

As far as the book jacket is concerned, you will be shown it for approval, but as a formality more than anything else, unless the right to approve jacket artwork is written into your contract (and publishers rarely agree to this – they feel they are in a better position to know what sort of jacket will sell your book than you are, which is probably true). You should check, however, that all the details are correct – including the 'blurb' on the back of the book. It has been known for publishers to get names wrong and just occasionally the story is totally unrecognisable.

Another time when you need to be alert to the possibility of mistakes is when you receive the proofs. Proofs are unbound copies of the final book and because all the typesetting has been done and the illustrations are in place it is important not to make any drastic changes (indeed your contract will probably make you liable for the cost if you do). But if you spot any mistakes, then speak up.

PUBLICATION

One thing that many new authors forget is that publication of a book doesn't happen instantly. The gap between an offer being made and actual publication is often as much as eighteen months to two years. It always makes me laugh when, around November time, I start receiving stories with a view to publication that Christmas! It just isn't humanly possible, I'm afraid.

You will receive an advance copy 'hot off the press' prior to publication of your book and, once it is actually on the bookshop shelves, you should receive complimentary – or 'gratis' – copies for your own distribution to family and friends. Do remember to keep at least a couple of copies of your book for yourself. It is unlikely, as a first book, that it will have a long shelf life and it could well be out of print within a few years. Once that happens, it will be impossible to get hold of more copies, and it's always good to be able to show future publishers samples of published work.

How well your book is marketed will depend on how good your publisher's marketing and sales teams are. The marketing team will promote your book in any way they think appropriate – first, by ensuring that it is included in their catalogue. Children's publishing catalogues generally come out on an annual basis and include all the books that will be published by them during that year.

The marketing team will also try to persuade all the relevant critics to review your work, although this isn't always easy with children's books, and even less easy for a new author.

The sales team will work on getting retail outlets to stock your books – although, again, this isn't always easy. Large book chains know that only the high-profile children's authors sell in any great quantities, so it may be a case of using persuasive powers or smaller bookshops and specialist children's bookshops.

There is a certain amount of promotion you can do yourself.

Contact local bookshops (who may be keen to stock your book if you are available for signing sessions and if your publisher can provide showcards), speak to local schools to arrange author visits, go to local libraries to arrange author visits, and send details of your book and yourself to local papers, radio stations and regional TV. The more you can promote yourself, the more copies of your book you are going to sell.

ROYALTIES

To start with, you won't earn any royalties because you'll still be earning your advance. However, you will receive royalty statements (twice a year usually, or as specified in your contract), which will show how quickly your advance is being earned. Once it has earned out, and assuming that your book is still selling, you will receive twice-yearly royalty cheques – but these may only be for a few pounds!

If you don't have an agent to check your royalty statements for you, check them carefully yourself. Again The Society of Authors can help with this task. If, after two years or so, the sales are very low, or down to nil, a reprint may well be in order. If not, ask your editor why not? A decision to reprint has to be taken with some care as far as the publisher is concerned and if, after discussion, they decided not to reprint, you can ask for the book rights to revert to you. Who knows – after several years, if the time is right, someone may be keen to bring out a new edition.

CHAPTER SEVENTEEN

HELP!

Writing is a very isolating experience. It doesn't matter how experienced you are – you will always feel, to a certain extent, alone. However, for children's writers, there is plenty of ongoing support available.

AGENTS

Many children's writers are desperate to enlist the help of an agent. This isn't, necessarily, because they feel that agents are the only route to success: more that they see agents as someone to relieve the loneliness of being a writer. They imagine them as being a combination of editor, therapist and friend all rolled into one. And they also believe that an agent will help them negotiate their way through the minefield of contracts – and find them a publisher in the first place.

These days, with fewer publishers being prepared to accept unsolicited manuscripts, there are more agents around who are prepared to take on unpublished writers; however, do remember that agents are *not* necessarily the answer to the new author's prayers. Even if you do persuade an agent to take you on, you will, until you have some experience and confidence in your own abilities, find that your agent is just another hoop to jump through. Under the terms of your agreement with your agent, you will almost certainly have to submit all work to publishers through him or her and, because as a new author you come low on their list of priorities, it can sometimes take an agent a long time to give you any sort of reaction to your work.

In the meantime, your hands are tied. And if, eventually, they come back to you with a negative response and refuse to submit your work to a publisher, you are completely stuck. You *have* to trust their judgement if you want to stay with them – but, on the other hand, you will be itching to submit your work to publishers, no matter what your agent says.

Nevertheless, if you find an agent you respect, you can build a creative and beneficial relationship. A good agent will devote time and energy to making your book as good as it can be. Once it reaches the publisher it will unquestionably be looked at with more speed than if it had simply joined the slush pile of unsolicited work. A good agent will also keep you in touch with current publishing requirements, which will, inevitably, put you ahead of the game. And the best agents will have the pulling power to be able to negotiate larger advances.

My advice would be not to waste time trying to find an agent until you have tried a few publishers first. Then I would suggest approaching a couple of agents and seeing what reaction you get.

If an agent does express an interest in taking you onto their list, do make sure that you meet them first, to assess whether or not you feel you could work closely with them. Check out their credentials and approach. Ask whether they are prepared to share their experience and creativity with authors, providing full editorial guidance, or whether they simply send manuscripts out to publishers 'untouched'. Ask how long they take, on average, to respond to authors with criticism and advice. Ask if they will regularly touch base with you to let you know of any developments, and to tell you what sort of books children's publishers are currently looking for. Ask if they will keep you informed about the submissions they make, and whether, once you have forged a relationship with a particular editor, they are happy for you to work with that person direct without using the agent as a 'go-between'. And – most importantly – ask what percentage they will demand should they sell your book! Leave no stone unturned – after all, you will be entrusting your precious work to this person, and you must be able to think that they are doing their very best for you.

Remember that there are a few unscrupulous agents out there who do not abide by a generally recognised code of practice. This code, set out by the Association of Authors' Agents (www.agentsassoc.co.uk), states that agents will not take money just to be an agent, only on commission. There have been several cases recently where agents have demanded large amounts of money from authors 'up front' and promised to approach a set number of publishers within a given timescale. Even if they do as they promise, it's not much good unless they have built up a relationship with the publishers they are approaching. At Puffin, I receive a large number of manuscripts from so-called 'agents' but, effectively, these are just unsolicited submissions accompanied by some fancy headed notepaper!

BOOKS

If you haven't done so already, there are several books I would suggest adding to your writer's library that will be of invaluable assistance to you:

The Children's Writers' & Artists' Yearbook (A & C Black).
This is the children's publishing version of the *The Writers' & Artists' Yearbook* and is updated annually. It has excellent articles on writing for children written by leading editors, agents and writers.

The Children's Writers' Handbook (Macmillan)
Most writers have one or the other of the above. However, if money is no object, I would suggest keeping both for reference purposes. In my opinion, *The Children's Writers' Handbook* isn't as comprehensive or extensive as *The Children's Writers' & Artists' Yearbook*.

The Rough Guide to Children's Books compiled by Nicholas Tucker (together with Julia Eccleshare for the teenage edition).
These wonderful pocket books come targeted at three age groups: 0–5 years, 5–11 years and teenage. They contain reviews of hundreds of books and although, obviously, not completely up to date, all three books give an excellent overview of the children's market.

Best Book Guide

This booklet is put together by Booktrusted (previously known as Young Book Trust) and is updated annually. It features a selection of titles – from Picture Books to teenage fiction – that have caught the eye of Booktrusted reviewers. For more information on this, and other guides produced by Booktrusted, visit www.booktrusted.com or tel. 020 8516 2977.

Ideas For Children's Writers by Pamela Cleaver (How To Books)

A comprehensive resourse book of plots, themes, genres, lists, what's hot and what's not.

What Do I Have To Do To Get A Book Published by Jo Anthony (www.indepublishing.com)

This book is packed with hints, tips and advice from successfully self-published authors, mainstream publishers, literary agents and a wide range of companies offering self-publishing services.

PUBLICATIONS

As well as books, there are a number of magazines on sale that are very helpful to the children's writer:

Writing Magazine and Writers' News

Writing Magazine is available monthly on the newsstands; *Writers' News*, from the same stable, is available by subscription only. Both contain interesting features on all aspects of writing, including articles specifically targeted at children's writers. They also contain information on writing circles and writing courses.

For subscription details, contact: *tel. 01778 392482 or visit www.writersnews.co.uk*

Books for Keeps

This is an excellent magazine aimed at everyone interested in children's books. It comes out bi-monthly and is full of book reviews, articles, authorgraphs etc. If you were going to subscribe to one magazine and no other, this is the one I would choose.

By subscription from: *Books for Keeps, 1 Effingham Road, London SE12 8NZ or visit www.booksforkeeps.co.uk*

Carousel

This magazine is similar to *Books for Keeps* except it is available three times a year (i.e. once a term) only.

By subscription from: *Carousel, The Saturn Centre, 54–76 Bissell Street, Birmingham B5 7HX or visit www.carouselguide.co.uk*

Reader's Review

Published by Troubador Publishing Ltd, this is available by subscription three times a year. It is basically a collection of independent reviews of self-published books but it also features helpful articles and tips on marketing your own work etc.

By subscription from: *Reader's Review Magazine, Troubador Publishing Ltd., 9 De Montfort Mews, Leicester LE1 7FW or visit www.troubador.co.uk/readersreviews*

The Bookseller

This magazine, available weekly from newsagents, is gradually becoming more orientated towards the children's books world. As well as the occasional round-up of children's publishing in a section entitled 'Children's Book News', it is also now producing a *Children's Bookseller* twice a year. It is expensive to buy on a weekly basis but if you can find out when the *Children's Bookseller* will be appearing, it might be worth ordering a copy of that particular edition. It also has a very good website: www.thebookseller.com

For details, contact: *The Bookseller, VNU Entertainment Media Ltd., 5th Floor, Endeavour House, 189 Shaftesbury Avenue, London WC2H 8TJ*

ORGANISATIONS

A number of organisations have been mentioned in passing throughout this book: here's more information on those that are most useful for the new writer.

Booktrust

Booktrust is the largest literature organisation in the United Kingdom. The Children's Literature Team offer advice and information on all aspects of children's reading and books.

Details from: *Booktrust, Book House, 45 East Hill, London SW18 2QZ or visit their website at www.booktrust.org.uk*

The Children's Book Circle (CBC)

This organisation provides a discussion forum for anybody interested in children's books. The CBC meets regularly and meetings are addressed by a panel of speakers on a chosen topic and usually take place at children's publishing houses in Central London.

Membership enquiries to: *Elv Moody, Children's Book Circle, Scholastic Ltd., Euston House, 24 Evershot Street, London NW1 1DB or visit www.childrensbookcircle.org.uk*

The Federation of Children's Book Groups

Like the Children's Book Circle, this is an organisation for all those involved in children's books. However, it has a more national flavour and organises a large annual conference.

Membership enquiries to: *Federation of Children's Book Groups, 2 Bridge Wood View, Horsforth, Leeds LS18 5PE or visit www.fcbg.org.uk*

Seven Stories, The Centre for Children's Books

This is the national home for children's literature and houses a unique and growing collection of manuscripts, artwork and other pre-publication material. Seven Stories provides the only exhibition space in the UK wholly dedicated to showcasing the incomparable legacy of British writing and illustrating for children.

The Centre can be found at: *30 Lime Street, Ouseburn Valley, Newcastle upon Tyne, NE1 2PQ or visit the website at www.seven stories.org.uk*

The Society of Authors

You will not be able to become a member of this society until you have had a formal publishing offer for a book. However, once this happens, it is a very useful organisation. As mentioned previously, it offers a free contract advisory service and also produces a journal, *The Author*, which is full of information, articles and publishing news.

Enquiries to: *The Society of Authors, 84 Drayton Gardens, London SW10 9SB or visit their website at www.societyofauthors.org*

TRAINING AND ADVICE

You can, of course, join a local writer's circle. These circles tend to meet on a regular basis and members take it in turns to read out their work. Personally, I wouldn't recommend this route unless the writing circle you choose specialises in children's writing. If other members know nothing about children's publishing, you will almost certainly get an inaccurate view of your work, which may harm, rather than help, any future success.

However, there are plenty of other places where you can go for training and advice.

The Arvon Foundation

This organisation offers writers the opportunity to live and work with professional authors. It runs a large variety of writing courses, including writing for children, at three centres in Devon, Yorkshire and Scotland. The accommodation tends to be on the basic – and over-crowded – side, but any discomfort is well worth enduring for the excellence of the course content.

Details from: *Arvon Foundation, Totleigh Barton, Sheepwash, Beaworthy, Devon EX21 5NS or visit their website at www.arvonfoundation.org*

The Children's Literature International Summer School

This is a biennial five-day event held at the University of Surrey Roehampton. It provides a forum in which participants and researchers in the field of children's literature can exchange ideas and broaden their knowledge of the subject. There is, also, an optional creative-writing module.

Details from: *University of Surrey Roehampton, Froebel College, London SW15 5PJ or visit their website at www.ncrcl.ac.uk*

The City Literary Institute

This is an adult education college and provides a wide variety of part-time writing courses for adult and children's writers.

Details from: *The City Literary Institute, 16 Stukeley Street, London WC2B 5LJ or visit www.citylit.ac.uk*

The Writers' Advice Centre for Children's Books

This organisation (run by me!) is the only one of its kind in the country. It is open to all-comers and offers individual editorial and marketing advice to children's writers on a fee-paying basis.

We have collected together a team of editorial readers, all of whom currently work in children's publishing, and we also run day courses , workshops and a home-study course.

Further details from: *The Writers' Advice Centre, 16 Smiths Yard, Summerley Street, London SW18 4HR. Tel. 0797 9905353 or visit our website at www.writersadvice.co.uk*

ONLINE RESOURCES

Achuka Children's Books
www.achuka.co.uk

The most up-to-date and comprehensive online guide to children's books and what's new in children's publishing. With author interviews, children's books news across the globe plus links to many other sites.

Armadillo
www.armadillomagazine.com

An online magazine about children's books, including reviews, interviews, features and profiles.

The Lion and the Unicorn website
www.lionunicornbooks.co.uk

The official website of The Lion and the Unicorn bookshop – a specialist children's bookshop based in Richmond. Here you can find out more about the bookshop and dip into their quarterly newsletter *THE ROAR!*. The site also features news, reviews, author events, services for schools, recommendations and bestsellers.

The Word Pool
www.wordpool.co.uk

An independent website that profiles authors of children's books and gives information and advice for aspiring writers. Also, access to a free monthly newsletter.

And Lastly . . .

A speaker on one of our Writers' Advice Centre courses recently brought me up short. He reminded us all that, no matter what books we read, no matter how many courses we go to, no matter how many publishers we speak to, the only people who really matter when we are writing for children are the children themselves.

So, as well as involving yourself in the children's book world, involve yourself with children. Expand your research to include books on child development and child psychology.

And always bear in mind that writing – any kind of writing – is a craft. Like all crafts, it takes time and hard work to perfect. I have seen many authors over the years and I have learnt, through experience, success isn't a question of talent – at least, not only talent. Above all, it's a question of perseverance.

A very famous artist, in his eighties and dying, was still working on a canvas. When asked what he was doing, he replied, 'I'm learning.' That's how it should be for you. A writer, like an artist, never stops learning, no matter what stage he or she is at. I truly believe that those authors who want to make it will do so in the end. It's a question of learning from experience, believing in your own abilities, and never, ever, giving up.

Good luck!

PRIZES AND AWARDS

I'm going to start with competitions for unpublished children's writers and then move on to mention some of the better known prizes and awards for published writers. These lists are, by no means, comprehensive and it is always worth keeping a look out for other competitions run by publishers, magazines and newspapers.

For example, at the time of going to press, Lion Children's Books had just finished running a Picture Book competition called *A Lion's Tale*. They were looking for a winning story of between 300–800 words with a prize of publication and £1000. *Writers' News* (see previous chapter) publish an annual competitions guide, which features a selection of prizes offered to new writers, many of them to new children's writers.

However, there is a dearth of quality writing competitions for the new writer. When Waterstones ran its Wow Factor competition last year in conjunction with Faber & Faber, they received 3,500 entries – so it should go without saying that the competition for prizes is fierce.

Competitions for Unpublished Children's Writers and Illustrators

Killie Writing Competition

This is an annual competition usually with three categories in the children's sector: 5–7-year-olds, 8–11-year-olds and 12–16-year-olds. Free expressive writing (poetry or fiction) with no limit on subject, word count, style or format. Various prizes with overall best entry receiving £1000 and a trophy.

Details: Killie Writing Competition, Kilmarnock College, KA3 7AT

Tel. 01355 302160

Web. www.killie.co.uk

London Writers' Competition

Only open to writers who live and work in the Greater London Area. Awards are made annually in four classes – poetry, short story, fiction for children and plays. Prizes total £1000 in each class.

Details: Arts Office, Wandsworth Council, Room 224a, Wandsworth Town Hall, High Street, London SW18 2PU

Tel. 020 8871 8711

Web. www.wandsworth.gov.uk/arts

Write a Story for Children Competition

Three prizes (1st £2000, 2nd £300, 3rd £200) are awarded annually for a short story for children, maximum 1000 words.

Details: The Academy of Children's Writers, PO Box 95, Huntingdon, Cambs PE28 5RL

Tel. 01487 832752

Web. www.childrens-writers.co.uk

The Writers' Advice Centre Story Competition

An annual competition to write a children's story for any age group of up to 1000 words on a set theme. First prize £100.

Details: The Writers' Advice Centre, 16 Smiths Yard, Summerley Street, London SW18 4HR

Tel. 0797 9905353

Web. www.writersadvice.co.uk

The Macmillan Prize for Children's Picture Book Illustration

Three prizes are awarded annually for unpublished children's book illustrations by art students in higher education establishments in the UK. Prizes: 1st £1000, 2nd £500, 3rd £250.
Details: Macmillan Children's Books, 20 New Wharf Road, London N1 9RR
Tel. 020 7014 6124

The Macmillan Writer's Prize for Africa

A biennial competition devoted to previously unpublished works of fiction by African writers from all over the continent. There are two awards for children's literature and teenage fiction, an award for the best new children's writer and an additional award for illustration.
Details: www.writeforafrica.com

Saga Children's Book Competition

A competition run by *Saga Magazine* in association with HarperCollins is looking for writers aged fifty and over who can write for older children. Completed manuscripts should be between 20,000–60,000 words. The winner will have their book published by HarperCollins.
Details: HarperCollins Children's Books, 77–85 Fulham Palace Road, London W6 8JB
Tel. 020 8307 4080
Web. www.saga.co.uk/magazine or www.harpercollins.co.uk

OTHER PRIZES AND AWARDS

This list of prizes and awards is not open to unpublished writers but it should still be of interest to anyone wishing to break into the children's publishing market. The children's book market is huge and, when trying to keep up with what is being published, it is sometimes hard to choose one book from another. A prize-winning book, on the other hand, is an immediate recommendation as more often than not these books have been selected by children themselves. For purposes of research, if you only read the twenty or so prize winners of the awards listed below, you would give yourself a very good grounding in what works well in children's publishing.

Angus Book Award

This is an initiative to encourage pupils to read quality teenage fiction. From January to March, third-year pupils read and assess the five shortlisted titles, chosen by teachers and librarians from books published in paperback in the preceding twelve months and written by an author resident in the UK. The books are discussed in class before the children vote in a secret ballot.

Current winner at: www.angus.gov.uk/bookaward

The *Blue Peter* Children's Book Awards

Awarded annually and judged by a panel of chidren and adults. There are three categories – The Book I Couldn't Put Down, The Best Illustrated Book to Read Aloud and The Best Book With Facts. Winners are announced in December on a *Blue Peter* special broadcast by CBBC.

Current winners at: www.bbc.co.uk/bluepeter

Booktrust Early Years Awards

The winners of each of three categories – Baby Book Award, Pre-School Award and Best New Illustrator – each receive £2000.

Current winners at: www.booktrusted.org.uk

The Booktrust Teenage Prize

The first annual national book prize to recognise and celebrate the best in young adult fiction. The author of the best book for teenagers receives £2500 and is chosen from a shortlist of six.

Current winner at: www.bookheads.org.uk

The Branford Boase Award

An annual award of £1000 is made to a first-time writer of a full-length children's novel (age group: 7+). The editor is also recognised.

Current winner at: www.branfordboaseaward.org.uk

British Book Awards

Referred to as the 'Nibbies' and presented annually, this includes the WHSmith Children's Book of the Year.

Current winner at: www.britishbookawards.com

The Children's Laureate

A biennial award of £10,000 to honour a writer or illustrator of children's books for a lifetime's achievement. The current Children's Laureate is Jacqueline Wilson and past winners have been Quentin Blake, Anne Fine and Michael Morpurgo.

The Carnegie Medal

The Carnegie Medal is given for an outstanding book for children. Contenders are appraised for characterisation, plot, style, accuracy, imaginative quality and that indefinable element that lifts the book above the competition.

Current winner at: www.ckg.org.uk

The Kate Greenaway Medal

This goes to an artist who has produced distinguished work in the illustration of children's books. The nominated books are assessed for design, format and production as well as artistic merit.

Current winner at: www.ckg.org.uk

Costa Book Awards (formerly The Whitbread Book Awards)

The awards celebrate and promote the most enjoyable contemporary British writing. There are five categories but only one for children's writing. The winner in each category receives £5000.

Current winner at: www.costabookawards.co.uk

The *Guardian* Children's Fiction Prize

The *Guardian* annual prize of £1500 is for a work of children's fiction for children over eight (no Picture Books). The winning book is chosen by the Children's Book Editor together with a team of three to four authors of children's books.

Current Winner at: www.guardian.co.uk

NASEN & *TES* Special Education Needs Book Award

These prizes are awarded to books that enhance the knowledge and understanding of those engaged in the education of children with special needs.

Current winners at: www.teachingexhibitions.co.uk

The Nestlé Children's Book Prize

Three prizes are awarded to three shortlisted books in each category: 5 and under, 6–8 years and 9–11 years. The award winners receive £2500 (Gold), £1500 (Silver) and £500 (Bronze).

Past winners at: www.booktrust.org.uk

North East Book Award

Awarded to a book first published in paperback between May and the end of June the following year. The shortlist is selected by librarians, teachers and the previous year's student judges, and the final winner by Year 10 students.

Joint winners in 2006 were *Looking for JJ* by Anne Cassidy (Scholastic) and *Roxy's Baby* by Catherine MacPhail (Bloomsbury).

Nottingham Children's Book Awards

Nottingham children choose their favourite four paperbacks of the year. The award is in four age groups – Foundation, 5–7 years, 8–9 years and 10–11 years.

Current winners at: www.nottinghamchildrensbookaward.co.uk

Ottaker's Children's Book Prize

This prize (£1000) celebrates exciting new or not yet established authors of children's books. It is unique in that booksellers and children select the shortlist and ultimate winner from books not yet published.

Winner in 2006 was *The Diamond of Drury Lane* by Julia Golding (Egmont).

The Red House Chilren's Book Award

This award is given annually to authors of works of fiction for children. It is divided into three categories – Younger Children,

Younger Readers and Older Readers. A 'Pick of the Year' book-list is published in conjunction with the award.

Current winners at: www.redhousechildrensbookaward.co.uk

Sheffield Children's Book Award

The Sheffield Children's Book Award is presented annually to the book chosen as the most enjoyable by the children of Sheffield. There are three Categories – Picture Books, Shorter Novels and Longer Novels.

Current winners at: www.sheffield.gov.uk

South Lanarkshire Book Award

This is an award for the best teenage book. The initial selection is by librarians and the final winner is chosen by a panel of school students.

Current winner at: www.slc-learningcentres.org.uk

BIBLIOGRAPHY

Ahlberg, Allan, *Heard it in the Playground*, (new ed.), Puffin Books, London: 1991

Ahlberg, Allan, *Please Mrs Butler*, (new ed.), Puffin Books, London: 2003

Allen, Linda, 'Mr Simkin's Bathtub', *The Puffin Book of Five-Minute Stories,* Perrault et. al, Puffin Books, London: 2000.

Bawden, Nina, *The Peppermint Pig*, (new ed.), Puffin Books, London: 1989

Blackman, Malorie, *Pig Heart Boy*, Young Corgi, London: 1998

Blackman, Malorie, *That New Dress*, Hodder Wayland, London: 1991

Blackman, Malorie, *Not So Stupid!*, Livewire Books for Teenagers, London: 1990

Blackman, Malorie, *Hacker*, Corgi Childrens, London: 1993

Blackman, Malorie, *That New Dress*, Hodder Wayland, London: 1991

Boyne, John, *The Boy in the Striped Pyjamas*, Doubleday, New York: 2006

Burchill, Julie, *Sugar Rush*, Macmillan's Children's Books, London: 2004

Burgess, Melvin, *Junk*, Andersen Press, London: 1996

Cave, Kathryn and Riddell, Chris, *Something Else*, (new ed.), Puffin Books, London: 1995

Cole, Babette, *Prince Cinders*, Hamish Hamilton, London: 1987

Cole, Babette, *Princess Smartypants*, Hamish Hamilton, London: 1987

Colfer, Eoin, *Benny and Omar*, O'Brien Press, Dublin: 2004

Dahl, Roald, *Matilda*, Jonathan Cape Children's Books, London: 1988

Doherty, Berlie, *Dear Nobody*, Hamish Hamilton, London: 1991

Donnelly, Jennifer, *A Gathering Light*, Bloomsbury, London: 2003

Drabble, Margaret, *The Millstone*, Penguin, London: 1968

Eames, Susan, 'Cold Feet', *The Puffin Book of Five-Minute Stories,* Perrault et al., Puffin Books, London: 2000

Ellis, Deborah, *The Breadwinner*, Oxford University Press: 2001

Fine, Anne, *Crummy Mummy and Me*, (new ed.), Puffin Books: 1989

Fine, Anne, *Flour Babies*, Hamish Hamilton, London: 1992

Fine, Anne, *Madame Doubtfire*, Hamish Hamilton, London: 1987

Finn Garner, James, *Politically Correct Bedtime Stories*, Souvenir Press, London: 1994

Geraghty, Margaret, *Novelist's Guide*, Piatkus Books, London: 1995

Gervais, Ricky, *Flanimals*, Faber and Faber, London: 2004

Gleitzman, Morris, *Bumface*, Viking, London: 1998

Grahame, Kenneth, *Wind in the Willows*, (new ed.), Penguin, London: 1994

Haddon, Mark, *The Curious Incident of the Dog in the Night-time*, Vinatage, London: 2004

Hammond, Richard, *Can You Feel the Force?*, Dorling Kindersley, London: 2006

Harvey, John, *What About it Sharon?*, Puffin, London: 1979

Hearn, Lian, *Across the Nightingale Floor*, Macmillan, London: 2002

Hinton, Nigel, *Time Bomb*, Puffin, London: 2005

Hornby, Nick, *A Long Way Down*, Viking, London: 2005

Howard, John, *The Key to Chintak*, Anthony Rowe Publishing Services: 2005

Hutchins, Pat, *Rosie's Walk*, Bodley Head Children's Books, London: 1968

Kay, Jackie, 'Sleekit', *Three Has Gone*, Puffin Books, London: 1996

King-Smith, Dick, *Clever Duck*, Viking Children's Books, London: 1996

King-Smith, Dick, *The Sheep Pig*, Puffin, London: 1995

Kipling, Rudyard, *Just So Stories*, (new ed.) Puffin Books, London: 1984

Knowles, Chris and Horsey, Julian, *The Paper Shoe Book*, Clarkson Potter, London: 1995

Laird, Elizabeth, *Kiss the Dust*, Heinemann Young Books, London: 1991

Leicester, Mal, *Special Stories for Disability Awareness*, Jessica Kingsley Publishers, London: 2006

Leicester, Mal, *Making Miracles*, Acebabes, London: 2001

Lewis, C.S., *The Chronicles of Narnia*, (new ed.), Collins, London: 2001

McCartney, Paul, *High in the Clouds: An Urban Furry Tail*, Faber Children's Books, London: 2005

McKee, David, *Not Now, Bernard*, (new ed.) Red Fox, London: 1996

MacPhail, Catherine, *Run Zan Run*, Bloomsbury, London: 2005

MacRae, Lindsay, 'High Noon at Barking Odeon', *You Canny Shove Yer Granny off a Bus!*, Viking, London: 1995

Madonna, *The English Roses*, Puffin, London: 2003

Magorian, Michelle, *Goodnight Mister Tom*, Viking Children's Books, London: 1981

Milne, A.A., *The House at Pooh Corner*, Mammoth, London: 1965

Milne, A.A., *Winnie the Pooh*, Heinemann Young Books, London: 1973

Minogue, Kylie, *Kylie: The Showgirl Princess*, Puffin Books, London: 2006

Morpurgo, Michael, *Muck and Magic: Stories from the Countryside*, Heinemann Young Books: 1995

Morrin, Stephen R., *The Day the Sky Fell Down*, Stephen R. Morrin, UK: 1998

Nesbit, E., *The Railway Children*, (new ed.), Penguin Books, London: 1995

Paton Walsh, Jill, *A Parcel of Patterns*, Viking Children's Books, London: 1983

Paul, Korky and Thomas, Valerie, *Winnie the Witch*, Oxford Univeristy Press: 1993

Pirani, Felix, *Abigail at the Beach*, Collins, London: 1998

Postgate, Daniel, *Kevin Saves the World*, Collins and Brown, London: 1999

Powling, Chris (ed.), *Best of Books for Keeps*, Bodley Head, London: 1994

Pullman, Philip, *The Amber Spyglass*, Scholastic, London: 2000

Ridley, Philip, *Krindlekrax*, Jonathan Cape Children's Books, London: 1991

Ridley, Philip, *Kasper in the Glitter*, Viking Children's Books, London: 1994

Ridley, Philip, *The Meteorite Spoon*, Viking Children's Books, London: 1994

Rosen, Michael and Oxenbury, Helen, *We're Going on a Bear Hunt*, Walker Books, London: 1989

Rossoff, Meg, *How I Live Now*, Puffin, London: 2004

Rowling, J.K., *Harry Potter and the Half-Blood Prince*, Bloomsbury, London: 2005

Rowling, J.K., *Harry Potter and the Philosopher's Stone*, Bloomsbury, London: 1998

Smith, Dodi, *I Capture the Castle*, (new ed.), Red Fox: London, 2003

Star Cooks, Dorling Kindersley, London: 2006

Swindell, Robert, *Stone Cold*, (new ed.), Puffin, London: 2005

Symes, Ruth, *The Master of Secrets*, Puffin, London: 1997

Taylor, G.P., *Shadowmancer*, Puffin, London: 2005

Tolkien, J.R.R, *Lord of the Rings*, HarperCollins (new ed.), London: 1995

Truss, Lynne, *Eats, Shoots and Leaves*, Profile, London: 2003

Umanksy, Kaye, *Romantic Giant*, Hamish Hamilton, London: 1994

Van Straten, Michael, *Super Juice for Kids*, Mitchell Beazley, London: 2006

Wegner, Fritz, *Heaven on Earth*, Walker Books: 1992

West, John, 'Ghost Train', *Simply Spooky: Ghost Stories*, Orion Children's Books, London: 1997

Wyndham, Lee, *Writing for Children and Teenagers*, Writer's Digest Books, London: 1991

Zephaniah, Benjamin, 'Once Upon a Time', *Talking Turkeys*, Puffin Books, London:1995

INDEX

Note: page numbers in **bold** refer to diagrams.